北大版短期培训汉语教材

博雅速成汉语

Boya Speed-up Chinese

第二册
Book 2

李晓琪　宋绍年　刘立新　章　欣　编著
by Li Xiaoqi　Song Shaonian　Liu Lixin　Zhang Xin

图书在版编目(CIP)数据

博雅速成汉语. 第二册/李晓琪等编著. —北京：北京大学出版社，2017.4
（北大版短期培训汉语教材）
ISBN 978-7-301-27930-4

Ⅰ.①博… Ⅱ.①李… Ⅲ.①汉语—对外汉语教学—教材 Ⅳ.①H195.4

中国版本图书馆CIP数据核字(2017)第002769号

书　　名	博雅速成汉语·第二册 BOYA SUCHENG HANYU·DI-ER CE
著作责任者	李晓琪　宋绍年　刘立新　章　欣　编著
责任编辑	崔　蕊　邓晓霞
标准书号	ISBN 978-7-301-27930-4
出版发行	北京大学出版社
地　　址	北京市海淀区成府路205号　100871
网　　址	http://www.pup.cn　新浪微博:@北京大学出版社
电子信箱	zpup@pup.pku.edu.cn
电　　话	邮购部 62752015　发行部 62750672　编辑部 62754144
印刷者	北京大学印刷厂
经销者	新华书店 720毫米×1020毫米　16开本　15印张　192千字 2017年4月第1版　2017年4月第1次印刷
定　　价	49.00元

未经许可，不得以任何方式复制或抄袭本书之部分或全部内容。
版权所有，侵权必究
举报电话：010-62752024　电子信箱：fd@pup.pku.edu.cn
图书如有印装质量问题，请与出版部联系，电话：010-62756370

Foreword

前　言

近年来,随着汉语国际推广事业的不断发展,越来越多的外国朋友希望学习汉语,了解中国,并且希望通过短时间的学习就能顺利地到中国旅游,能与中国人谈话聊天,能和中国开展一定的贸易活动。为达此目的,我们在编写《博雅速成汉语》时以第二语言教材编写理念为指导,以方便学习者为目的,力争使之成为一套适应时代需求的新速成汉语学习教材。

编写第二语言学习教材,一般的做法是,口语课本多以话题情景为纲,语言知识为辅;精读课本则多以语言知识为纲,兼顾功能。前者容易忽略语言知识的系统性,后者容易忽略语言材料的实用性。本套教材努力克服上述两方面的不足,尝试把二者有机地结合起来,在以话题情景为纲组织教材内容的同时,探索功能和结构相融合的编写模式,使学习者通过学习本套教材,既掌握扎实的语言基础知识,又掌握实用的听说技能。本套教材参照《新汉语水平考试大纲》,学生学完第一册,可以达到HSK二级水平;学完第二册,可以达到HSK三级水平;学完第三册,基本可以达到HSK四级水平。

本套教材把日常生活用语分成了15个话题:(1)问候和介绍;(2)学校生活;(3)问路和旅游;(4)时间和日期;(5)交通;(6)在旅馆;(7)访问和做客;(8)购物;(9)季节和天气;(10)健康和医疗;(11)饮食;(12)讨论问题;(13)兴趣爱好;(14)贸易;(15)学习汉语。全套书共三册,每册15课,共计45课。每课学习一个话题的部分用语。每册为一个循环。第一册的15课是15个话题中最基本的内容,掌握了它,就可以完成简单的汉语交际。后两册在此基础上逐渐加以扩展,使每个话题得以丰富和深化。其中第三册还有意识地加入了一些商业贸易用语,以增加本书的实用性。每课设有句型、课文、注释、语法、练习、生词等项目。每课的课文都包括对话,以训练听说能力;同时还设有叙述体短文,以训练阅读和理解语篇的能力。全部课文配有英文翻译。三册课文中的全部对话语体和第一册的叙述体短文标注了汉语拼音。课文和句型配有简明实用的注释,用以讲解语法知识。每课安排10个句型,20个左右生词,三册共450个句型,约900个生词。本套教材在词语和语言点的安排上注意体现重现和渐进的原则,以便于学习者学习。每课备有练习参考答案。此外,本套教材还在第一册安排了学习辅助资料,包括:语音基本知识、常用反义单音节形容词和常用俗语。

为引起学习者的兴趣,每册书后都配有三至四首古诗。

本套教材适用于在校学生的课堂教学,按照每周两课的进度,八周学完一册书。教师可以根据学习的期限和学习者的水平自由选择其中的一册(一个循环)进行教学。本套教材也可以用作会话手册,供学习汉语的各界人士自学之用。

本教材课文部分由曹莉、王舒翼女士翻译,特此致谢!

作者
2016年于北大燕园

Contents

目 录

1 他是哪国人？ ··· 1
　Where Does He Come From?

2 今天几号？ ··· 15
　What's the Date Today?

3 我有四门课 ··· 32
　I Have Got Four Subjects

4 动物园在马路南边 ··· 46
　The Zoo Is on the Southern Side of the Road

5 我买去上海的火车票 ··· 61
　 I Want to Buy a Train Ticket to Shanghai

6 中餐厅在一楼 ··· 75
　The Chinese Restaurant Is on the First Floor

7 你的家真漂亮 ··· 90
　Your House Is Really Beautiful

8 这件衣服很漂亮 ··· 104
　This Dress Is Very Pretty

9 你最喜欢哪个季节？ ··· 117
　Which Season Do You Like Best?

10 去医院看看病吧！ ·· 133
　 Go to See a Doctor Then!

11 鱼的味道怎么样？ ·· 149
　 How Is the Taste of the Fish?

12 你可以试试喝减肥茶 ·· 164
   You Can Try the Diet Tea

13 他是一个体育爱好者 ·· 179
   He Is a Sport Enthusiast

14 希望以后继续合作 ·· 193
   Wish We Would Further Our Cooperation in the Future

15 我的中文进步很快 ·· 209
   My Chinese Standard Improves Rapidly

生词总表 / 222
Vocabulary

附录　古诗三首 / 229
Appendix　Three Ancient Poems

1. Tā shì nǎ guó rén?
他是哪国人?
Where Does He Come From?

句型 | Sentence Patterns

1. 您早!
   Nín zǎo!
   Good morning!

2. 早上 好! 休息得好吗?
   Zǎoshang hǎo! Xiūxi de hǎo ma?
   Good morning! Did you have a good rest?

3. 您贵姓?
   Nín guìxìng?
   What is your surname?

4. 她姓李, 叫李英。
   Tā xìng Lǐ, jiào Lǐ Yīng.
   Her surname is Li. She is Li Ying.

5. 他是谁?
   Tā shì shuí?
   Who is he?

6. 他是我们公司的老板马丁先生。
Tā shì wǒmen gōngsī de lǎobǎn Mǎdīng xiānsheng.

He is our boss, Mr. Martin.

7. 他是哪国人?
Tā shì nǎ guó rén?

Where does he come from?

8. 他是美国人。
Tā shì Měiguórén.

He is an American.

9. 他懂几种语言?
Tā dǒng jǐ zhǒng yǔyán?

How many languages does he know?

10. 除了英语以外,他还懂德语、法语、日语和汉语。
Chúle Yīngyǔ yǐwài, tā hái dǒng Déyǔ、 Fǎyǔ、 Rìyǔ hé Hànyǔ.

Besides English, he knows German, French, Japanese and Chinese.

1 他是哪国人?
Where Does He Come From?

课文 | Text

(一)（宾馆里的对话 A dialogue in a hotel）

男： 您早!
Nín zǎo!
Good morning!

女： 早上好! 休息得好吗?
Zǎoshang hǎo! Xiūxi de hǎo ma?
Good morning! Did you have a good rest?

男： 很好，谢谢!
Hěn hǎo, xièxie!
Yes, very good. Thank you!

女： 请问，您是英国人吗?
Qǐngwèn, nín shì Yīngguórén ma?
Excuse me, are you from England?

男： 不，我不是英国人，我是美国人。
Bù, wǒ bú shì Yīngguórén, wǒ shì Měiguórén.
No, I am not from England. I am an American.

女： 对不起，请原谅。
Duìbuqǐ, qǐng yuánliàng.
I am sorry.

男：没 什么。您 贵姓?
Méi shénme. Nín guìxìng?

It is all right. What is your surname?

女：我 姓 李。
Wǒ xìng Lǐ.

My surname is Li.

男：你会说 英语 吗?
Nǐ huì shuō Yīngyǔ ma?

Can you speak English?

女：我 会 说 一点儿。
Wǒ huì shuō yìdiǎnr.

I know a little English.

男：别的 呢?
Biéde ne?

Anything else?

女：除了英语以外, 我还 能 说 一点儿 日语。
Chúle Yīngyǔ yǐwài, wǒ hái néng shuō yìdiǎnr Rìyǔ.

Besides English, I can speak a little Japanese.

男：因为 很 多客人都 说 英语和日语吧?
Yīnwèi hěn duō kèrén dōu shuō Yīngyǔ hé Rìyǔ ba?

Is it because many guests here speak English or Japanese?

女：是。
Shì.

Yes.

1 他是哪国人?
Where Does He Come From?

(二)

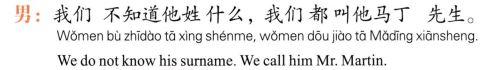

女: 他是谁?
Tā shì shuí?
Who is he?

男: 他是我们公司的老板。
Tā shì wǒmen gōngsī de lǎobǎn.
He is our boss.

女: 他姓什么?
Tā xìng shénme?
What is his family name?

男: 我们不知道他姓什么,我们都叫他马丁先生。
Wǒmen bù zhīdào tā xìng shénme, wǒmen dōu jiào tā Mǎdīng xiānsheng.
We do not know his surname. We call him Mr. Martin.

女: 马丁先生是哪国人?
Mǎdīng xiānsheng shì nǎ guó rén?
Where does Mr. Martin come from?

男: 他是美国人。
Tā shì Měiguórén.
He is an American.

女: 他会说汉语吗?
Tā huì shuō Hànyǔ ma?
Does he speak Chinese?

男：会。他懂很多种语言。汉语、日语、德语、
　　Huì. Tā dǒng hěn duō zhǒng yǔyán. Hànyǔ、 Rìyǔ、 Déyǔ、

法语他都会说。
Fǎyǔ tā dōu huì shuō.

Yes. He knows many languages. He can speak Chinese, Japanese, German and French.

（三）我的老师 My teacher

我的汉语老师是中国人。她姓李，叫李英。她身体很好，什么病也没有。她很喜欢喝茶，每天要喝七八杯。她说，喝茶对身体很有好处。李老师懂很多种语言。她的英语说得很好。除了英语，她还能说法语、德语和日语。李老师还很喜欢读书，她对英国历史和日本历史都很了解，她也很了解法国的文学。我们都非常喜欢李老师。

My Chinese language teacher is a Chinese. Her family name is Li and the full name is Li Ying. She is very healthy without any illness. She likes tea very much and drinks seven or eight cups each day. She says drinking tea is very good for health. Mrs. Li knows many languages. She speaks very good English. Besides that, she can speak French, German and Japanese. Mrs. Li likes reading too. She has good knowledge about the history of England and Japan. She also knows a lot about French literature. All of us like her very much.

1 他是哪国人?
Where Does He Come From?

注释 | Annotation

1. 您贵姓? What is your surname, please?

这是客气的问法,意思是:"您姓什么?"

"您贵姓" is a polite way of asking what your surname is.

2. 他是谁? Who is he?

"谁"(shuí)口语中一般读作"shéi"。

"谁"(shuí) is usually read as "shéi" in colloquial Chinese.

语法 | Grammar

1. 除了……以外,……还(也)

这是一个固定用法,"以外"可以省略不说。如:

This is a fixed structure and "以外" can be omitted. For example:

(1) 除了我,他也去过那儿。

　　Besides me, he has also been there.

(2) 除了红茶,我还喜欢喝绿茶。

　　Besides black tea, I also like green tea.

2. 表示疑问时，"谁"在句子中的位置有两种：

（1）在动词后："他是谁？""你喜欢谁？"

（2）在动词前："谁是美国人？""谁喜欢古典音乐？"

When "谁" is used in questions, it can be put:

（1）after the verb: "他是谁？""你喜欢谁？"

（2）before the verb: "谁是美国人？""谁喜欢古典音乐？"

练习 | Exercises

1. 听录音，选择合适的回答：

Listen to the record and choose a proper answer:

（1）A. 很好，谢谢！

　　B. 休息得好。

　　C. 不休息好。

（2）A. 我不英国人。

　　B. 我也是英国人。

　　C. 我是美国人。

（3）A. 没什么。

　　B. 原谅。

　　C. 不客气。

（4）A. 我贵姓李。

　　B. 贵姓李。

　　C. 我姓李。

1 他是哪国人？
Where Does He Come From?

(5) A. 我一点儿会说。
　　B. 我会一点儿说。
　　C. 我会说一点儿。

2. 连线：

Connect column A and column B:

A	B
他是哪国人？	他懂五种语言。
他懂几种语言？	他是我的汉语老师。
你休息得好吗？	他是英国人。
你的老师喜欢喝茶吗？	我会说法语，也会说英语。
他是谁？	我休息得很好，谢谢。
你会说法语吗？	他很喜欢喝茶。

3. 完成对话：

Complete the following dialogues:

(1) A：请问，您贵姓？
　　B：＿＿＿＿＿＿＿＿＿＿＿＿＿＿＿。
　　A：您是哪国人？
　　B：＿＿＿＿＿＿＿＿＿＿＿＿＿＿＿。
　　A：您会说汉语吗？
　　B：＿＿＿＿＿＿＿＿＿＿＿＿＿＿＿。

(2) A：您身体好吗？
　　B：＿＿＿＿＿＿＿＿＿＿＿＿＿＿＿，你呢？

A：_____。

B：你是不是中国人？

A：不，_____。

A：你的汉语说得很好。

(3) A：她是谁？

B：_____。

A：她懂汉语吗？

B：_____。

A：别的语言呢？

B：_____。（除了……）

(4) A：早上好！

B：早上好！_____？

A：我休息得很好。

B：_____，_____？

A：是的，我要去银行。

B：_____。

4. 改正病句：

Correct the mistakes in the following sentences:

(1) 我认识你很高兴也。

(2) 他我的老师。

(3) 他会说英语，会说日语还。

(4) 我的日语说不太好。

(5) 你的老师哪国人？

1 他是哪国人？
Where Does He Come From?

(6) 除了中国，我去过日本。
(7) 除了汉语，也我会日语。
(8) 你休息好吗？

5. **用下列词语说一段话：**

   Make a speech with the following words:

   题目：我的老师/我的老板

   参考词语：国　很　喜欢　会　除了……

生词 | New Words

1	早	zǎo	（形）	early	您早。/ Good morning.
2	早上	zǎoshang	（名）	morning	今天早上 / this morning 早上好。/ Good morning. 我早上八点到北京。 I will arrive at Beijing at eight a.m.
3	姓	xìng	（动）	surname	我姓王。 My surname is Wang. 老师姓李。 The teacher's surname is Li. 他姓什么？ What's his family name?
4	贵姓	guìxìng		(polite) surname	请问，您贵姓？ What's you surname, please?

5	她	tā	(代)	she; her	她是谁？/ Who is she? 她叫什么？ What's her name? 她是王红。 She is Wang Hong.
6	谁	shuí	(代)	who; whom	他是谁？/ Who is he? 你的汉语老师是谁？ Who is your Chinese teacher? 谁喜欢流行音乐？ Who loves pop music?
7	老板	lǎobǎn	(名)	boss	他是老板。/ He is the boss. 我们公司的老板是李先生。 Mr. Li is the boss of our company.
8	国	guó	(名)	country; nation	出(chū, go out)国 go abroad 美国 / the USA 他是哪国人？ What's his nationality?
9	语言	yǔyán	(名)	language	几种语言 / several languages 学习语言 / learn languages 你懂几种语言？ How many languages can you speak?
10	除了	chúle	(介)	besides	除了英语外，我还懂德语。 Besides English, I also know German. 除了大卫，我也喜欢音乐。 Besides David, I also love music. 除了双人间，还有单人间。 There're single rooms as well as double rooms.
11	原谅	yuánliàng	(动)	to forgive	请原谅。/ Sorry. 原谅我吧。 Please forgive me. 对不起，请原谅。 I'm very sorry.

1 他是哪国人？
Where Does He Come From?

12	多	duō	（形）	many	特别多 / lots of 单人间不多了。 There're not many single rooms. 外面有很多出租车。 There're a lot of taxis out there.
13	客人	kèrén	（名）	guest	一位客人 / a guest 很多客人 / many guests 请问，一共有几位客人？ Excuse me, how many guests altogether?
14	天	tiān	（名）	day	每天 / every day 我每天都说汉语。 I speak Chinese every day. 他每天要喝七八杯茶。 He drinks seven or eight cups of tea every day.
15	好处	hǎochù	（名）	benefit	学中文的好处 benefit of learning Chinese 懂几种外语很有好处。 It is very useful to know several foreign languages. 喝茶对身体很有好处。 Tea is very good for our health.

专有名词：

Proper nouns:

1	李英	Lǐ Yīng	name of a person
2	美国人	Měiguórén	American
3	英语	Yīngyǔ	English
4	德语	Déyǔ	German
5	法语	Fǎyǔ	French

6	日语	Rìyǔ	Japanese
7	英国人	Yīngguórén	English
8	英国	Yīngguó	England
9	日本	Rìběn	Japan
10	法国	Fǎguó	France

听力录音文本及参考答案

1. （1）早上好！休息得好吗？

    （2）请问，您是英国人吗？

    （3）对不起，请原谅。

    （4）您贵姓？

    （5）你会说英语吗？

    （1）A　（2）C　（3）A　（4）C　（5）C

2. 他是哪国人？——他是英国人。

    他懂几种语言？——他懂五种语言。

    你休息得好吗？——我休息得很好，谢谢。

    你的老师喜欢喝茶吗？——他很喜欢喝茶。

    他是谁？——他是我的汉语老师。

    你会说法语吗？——我会说法语，也会说英语。

3. 略。

4. （1）认识你我也很高兴。

    （2）他是我的老师。

    （3）他会说英语，还会说日语。

    （4）我的日语说得不太好。

    （5）你的老师是哪国人？

    （6）除了中国，我还去过日本。

    （7）除了汉语，我也会日语。

    （8）你休息得好吗？

5. 略。

2 今天几号?
Jīntiān jǐ hào?
What's the Date Today?

| 句型 | Sentence Patterns |

11. 你 每天 早上 几点起 床?
Nǐ měi tiān zǎoshang jǐ diǎn qǐ chuáng?
What time do you get up every morning?

12. 我 每天 早上 六点三刻起床。
Wǒ měi tiān zǎoshang liù diǎn sān kè qǐ chuáng.
I get up at a quarter to seven every morning.

13. 晚上 一般十一点半 睡觉。
Wǎnshang yìbān shíyī diǎn bàn shuì jiào.
I usually sleep at half past eleven at night.

14. 中午 大约十二点半 吃饭。
Zhōngwǔ dàyuē shí'èr diǎn bàn chī fàn.
I have lunch around half past twelve at noon.

15. 今天（是）几号?
Jīntiān (shì) jǐ hào?
What's the date today?

16. 今天（是）八月二十五号。
    Jīntiān (shì) bāyuè èrshíwǔ hào.

    Today is August 25th.

17. 他的生日是哪天？
    Tā de shēngrì shì nǎ tiān?

    When is his birthday?

18. 他的生日是五月二十五号。
    Tā de shēngrì shì wǔyuè èrshíwǔ hào.

    His birthday is on May 25th.

19. 他是一九九六年五月二十五日出生的。
    Tā shì yī jiǔ jiǔ liù nián wǔyuè èrshíwǔ rì chūshēng de.

    He was born on May 25th, 1988.

20. 他今年二十岁。
    Tā jīnnián èrshí suì.

    He is twenty years old this year.

2 今天几号?
What's the Date Today?

课文 | Text

(一)

女: 你每天早上几点起床?
Nǐ měi tiān zǎoshang jǐ diǎn qǐ chuáng?
What time do you get up every morning?

男: 我每天早上六点三刻起床。
Wǒ měi tiān zǎoshang liù diǎn sān kè qǐ chuáng.
I get up at a quarter to seven every morning.

女: 你起得很早,晚上几点钟睡觉?
Nǐ qǐ de hěn zǎo, wǎnshang jǐ diǎnzhōng shuì jiào?
You get up so early. What time do you go to bed at night?

男: 一般十一点半睡觉。
Yìbān shíyī diǎn bàn shuì jiào.
I usually sleep at half past eleven.

女: 中午 休息吗?
Zhōngwǔ xiūxi ma?

Do you take a rest at noon?

男: 中午 没有时间休息。十二点半吃饭，一点
Zhōngwǔ méiyǒu shíjiān xiūxi. Shí'èr diǎn bàn chī fàn, yī diǎn

半开始工作。
bàn kāishǐ gōngzuò.

There is no time for a rest at noon. I have lunch at half past twelve and the work continues at half past one p.m..

女: 我喜欢 中午休息一会儿。
Wǒ xǐhuan zhōngwǔ xiūxi yíhuìr.

I would like a short break at noon.

男: 是睡午觉吗?
Shì shuì wǔjiào ma?

Is it an afternoon nap?

女: 是，吃完 中午 饭，我要睡一会儿。
Shì, chīwán zhōngwǔ fàn, wǒ yào shuì yíhuìr.

Yes, I would have a nap after lunch.

男: 睡多长 时间?
Shuì duō cháng shíjiān?

How long do you nap then?

女: 大约半个小时。
Dàyuē bàn gè xiǎoshí.

About half an hour.

2 今天几号?
What's the Date Today?

男： 我也喜欢吃完饭睡一会儿，不过是在星期天。
Wǒ yě xǐhuan chīwán fàn shuì yíhuìr, búguò shì zài Xīngqītiān.
I also like a nap after the meal, but it is only on Sundays.

(二)

女： 今天几号?
Jīntiān jǐ hào?
What's the date today?

男： 今天八月二十五号。
Jīntiān bāyuè èrshíwǔ hào.
It is August 25th.

女： 你们学校快开学了吧?
Nǐmen xuéxiào kuài kāi xué le ba?
Is your school opening soon?

男： 是，九月一号开学。
Shì, jiǔyuè yī hào kāi xué.
Yes, it starts on September 1st.

女： 一个学期有多长?
Yí gè xuéqī yǒu duō cháng?
How long does a semester last?

男： 大约四个月，十六个星期。
Dàyuē sì gè yuè, shíliù gè xīngqī.
About four months, sixteen weeks.

女：太长了，一月才放假。
Tài cháng le, yīyuè cái fàng jià.
It is too long. The vacation will have to be waited till January.

男：我们每年都是一月十几号才放假。
Wǒmen měi nián dōu shì yīyuè shíjǐ hào cái fàng jià.
Our vacation always starts around the 10th of January every year.

（三）他二十岁 He is twenty years old

马学文是一九九六年五月二十五日出生的。今天是五月二十一日，他的生日快要到了。他特别高兴，因为今年的五月二十五日是他二十岁生日。那天是一个星期天，学校不上课。他打算先去参观一个博物馆，然后去公园，晚上请几位朋友去他家。他七点钟在家等他们。

Ma Xuewen was born on May 25th, 1996. It is May 21st today. His birthday is coming soon. He is especially happy because the 25th of May this year will be his twentieth birthday. It is on Sunday, and there is no class. He plans to go to visit a museum first, then go to the park, and then invite a few friends to his place in the evening. He will wait for them at seven o'clock at home.

2 今天几号?
What's the Date Today?

注释 | Annotation

1. 他的生日是五月二十五号。 His birthday is on May 25th.

"号"也可以说成"日","日"比较正式,"号"用于口语。

"号" can be also said to be "日", which is more formal. "号" is used in colloquial Chinese.

  一日（号）   first (1st)
  二日（号）   second (2nd)
  十一日（号）   eleventh (11th)
  十九日（号）   nineteenth (19th)
  二十日（号）   twentieth (20th)
  三十一日（号） thirty-first (31st)

2. 一九九六年五月二十五日　May 25th, 1996

在汉语中,表示年、月、日连用时的顺序是从年到月,再到日（号）。如：

The way to express a date in Chinese is YY-MM-DD. For example:

2013年8月15日/二〇一三年八月十五日

Aug. 15th, 2013

3. 今天几号? What's the date today?

是"今天是几号"的简略说法。口语常用。

A simplified form of "今天是几号", commonly used in colloquial Chinese.

4. 我也喜欢吃完饭睡一会儿，不过是在星期天。I also like a nap after the meal, but it is only on Sundays.

"不过"的意思与"可是"相同，但是程度比"可是"轻，且多用于口语。

The meaning of "不过" is similar to that of "可是", but the former suggests a tone of lighter degree than the latter. It's usually used in oral Chinese.

语法 | Grammar

1. 月份表示法　Indication of the months

一月	January	二月	February
三月	March	四月	April
五月	May	六月	June
七月	July	八月	August
九月	September	十月	October
十一月	November	十二月	December

2 今天几号?
What's the Date Today?

2. 年份表示法　Indication of year

2000年	二〇〇〇年	the year 2000
2005年	二〇〇五年	the year 2005
2011年	二〇一一年	the year 2011
2015年	二〇一五年	the year 2015

3. 才

副词"才"表示动作进行得慢、发生得晚。如：

Adverb "才" indicates actions take place slowly and late. For example:

（1）你为什么才做了三个练习？

　　Why have you done only three exercises?

（2）他每天十点才起床。

　　He does not get up until ten o'clock every day.

4. 一个学期有多长？

"多"用在表示上限的形容词前，询问程度。如：

"多" is used before adjectives indicating limits to inquire about the degree. For example:

（1）有多大

　　how big

（2）有多冷

　　how cold

（3）有多贵

　　how expensive

5. 是……的

"是……的"可以用来强调时间，被强调的时间放在"是……的"的中间。如：

"是……的" can be used for time emphasis. The time emphasized is placed between "是……的". For example:

(1) 马学文是一九九六年五月二十五日出生的。

　　Ma Xuewen was born on May 25th, 1996.

(2) 音乐会是下午三点的。

　　The concert is at 3∶00 p.m..

(3) 去上海的火车是晚上七点五十分的。

　　The train to Shanghai is at 7∶50 p.m..

练习 | Exercises

1. 听录音，判断对错：

Listen to the record and judge whether the statements are correct or not:

(1) 我每天六点四十五分起床。　☐

(2) 我十二点吃午饭。　☐

(3) 中午可以休息一会儿。　☐

(4) 我睡午觉。　☐

(5) 我每天都睡午觉。　☐

2 今天几号？
What's the Date Today?

2. 替换练习：

Substitution exercises:

（1）他的生日是<u>三月</u><u>二十一</u>日（号）。
　　　　　　　一　十五
　　　　　　　四　二
　　　　　　　八　二十
　　　　　　　二　八

（2）今天是<u>七月</u><u>十七</u>日，<u>星期二</u>。
　　　　　二　十一　　星期一
　　　　　五　一　　　星期日
　　　　　九　十九　　星期六
　　　　　十　二十一　星期五

（3）一个学期有多长？
　　　图书馆　　　大
　　　天气　　　　冷
　　　咖啡　　　　浓
　　　橘子　　　　甜

（4）<u>马学文</u>是<u>一九九六年五月二十五日</u><u>出生</u>的。
　　　我　　　十一点　　　　　睡觉
　　　他　　　六点　　　　　　起床
　　　他们　　八点钟　　　　　来我家
　　　我们　　今年九月　　　　来中国

3. 读出下列日期：

Read out the following dates:

(1) 18 日   2 月   1956 年
(2) 10 月   1 日   1949 年
(3) 25 日   1997 年   5 月
(4) 2008 年   星期二   1 号   4 月
(5) 星期四   2010 年   19 日   12 月

4. 用线段连接相关的上下句：

Match the questions with proper answers:

(1) 你每天早上几点起床？   A. 今天是四月二号。
(2) 一个学期有多长？   B. 一般十一点半睡觉。
(3) 你晚上几点睡觉？   C. 大约十二点半吃饭。
(4) 你中午几点吃饭？   D. 一九九六年。
(5) 今天几号？   E. 十月三号。
(6) 他的生日是哪天？   F. 我每天六点三刻起床。
(7) 他是哪一年出生的？   G. 大概四个月，十六个星期。

5. 选词填空：

Fill in the following blanks with the given words:

每个   每天   每星期   每年   每位   每间

(1) 他（   ）七点起床。
(2) 我（   ）都去拜访老师。
(3) （   ）老师都会说英语。

2 今天几号?
What's the Date Today?

(4) 我们（　　）都是一月放假。
(5) 他们（　　）有二十个小时课。
(6) （　　）房间都住满了。
(7) 他（　　）博物馆都去过。

6. 选词填空：

Fill in the following blanks with the given words:

因为　请　上课　然后　生日　特别　出生　参观

我是一九九六年五月二十五日 (1) 的。今天是五月二十一日，我的 (2) 快要到了。我 (3) 高兴，(4) 今年的五月二十五日是我二十岁生日。那天是一个星期天，学校不 (5) 。我打算先去 (6) 一个博物馆，(7) 去公园，晚上 (8) 几位朋友来我家。

7. 用下列词语说一段话：

Make a speech with the following words:

题目：我的一天

参考词语：一般　起床　吃饭　睡觉　开始　大约　喜欢

生词 | New Words

1	起床	qǐ chuáng		to get up	几点起床 when to get up 你早上几点起床？ When do you get up in the morning? 我每天六点起床。 I get up at 6 every day.
2	一般	yìbān	（副）	normally; usually	我一般六点起床。 Normally I get up at 6. 银行一般每天都开门。 Usually the bank is open every day. 我星期六一般不在家。 Normally, I'm out on Saturdays.
3	睡觉	shuì jiào		to go to bed; to sleep	十二点睡觉 go to bed at 12 o'clock 你每天几点睡觉？ When do you go to bed every day? 十二点睡觉太晚了。 It's too late to go to bed at 12.
4	大约	dàyuē	（副）	about; approximately	大约十点睡觉 go to bed at about ten 大约三十个人 about thirty people 我每天早上大约六点起床。 I get up at about 6 every morning.
5	日	rì	（名）	day	星期日 / Sunday 六月十三日 / June, 13th 今天是六月八日。 It's June 8th today.

2 今天几号?
What's the Date Today?

6	生日	shēngrì	(名)	birthday	今天是我的生日。 Today is my birthday. 你的生日是哪天? When is your birthday? 我的生日是十月三号。 October 3rd is my birthday.
7	月	yuè	(名)	month	六月 / June 十二月三日 / Dec. 3rd 我的生日在十月。 My birthday is in October.
8	出生	chūshēng	(动)	to be born	你是哪年出生的? When were you born? 我是一九八八年出生的。 I was born in 1988. 我是在北京出生的。 I was born in Beijing.
9	今年	jīnnián	(名)	this year	今年三月我要去中国。 I'm going to China this March. 今年我要学汉语。 I want to learn Chinese this year. 他是今年三月来北京的。 He came to Beijing this March.
10	岁	suì	(量)	year	十八岁 / 18 years old 六十岁 / 60 years old 我今年二十五岁。 I'm 25 years old this year.
11	开始	kāishǐ	(动)	to begin	开始上课。/ Class begins. 几点开始? When does it begin? 我是二〇〇七年开始学汉语的。 I started to learn Chinese in 2007.

12	工作	gōngzuò	(动)	to work	在中国工作 / work in China 我一点半开始工作。 My work begins at half past one. 你星期天也工作吗？ Do you work on Sundays?
13	完	wán	(动)	to be finished	吃完了 / dinner finished 看完了 reading/watching finished 吃完中午饭，我要睡一会儿。 I often have a nap after lunch.
14	长	cháng	(形)	long	很长时间 / long time 多长时间 / how much time 一个学期有十六个星期，太长了。 A semester consists of 16 weeks. It's so long.
15	不过	búguò	(连)	but	我喜欢吃完饭睡一会儿，不过是在星期天。 I like to have a nap after meal, but only on Sundays. 今天天气不错，不过有点儿冷。 Fine weather today, but a little cold. 我认识他，不过他不认识我。 I know him, but he doesn't know me.
16	才	cái	(副)	only	现在才八点。 It's only 8 o'clock now. 我才睡了一个小时。 I've only slept for one hour. 你怎么才来？ Why are you so late?

2 今天几号？
What's the Date Today?

| 17 | 请 | qǐng | （动） | to invite | 请朋友去我家。
Invite some frineds to my house.
晚上我请了几位朋友。
I've invited some friends tonight.
朋友请我星期六去参观博物馆。
My friends invite me to visit the museum on Saturday. |

专有名词：

Proper noun:

| 马学文 | Mǎ Xuéwén | name of a person |

听力录音文本及参考答案

1. （1）我每天早上六点三刻起床。
   （2）中午大约十二点半吃饭。
   （3）中午没有时间休息。
   （4）吃完中午饭，我要睡一会儿。
   （5）我也喜欢吃完饭睡一会儿，不过是在星期天。
   　（1）√　（2）×　（3）×　（4）√　（5）×

2. 略。

3. 略。

4. （1）F　（2）G　（3）B　（4）C　（5）A　（6）E　（7）D

5. （1）每天　　（2）每星期/每年　（3）每个/每位　（4）每年
   （5）每星期　（6）每个/每间　（7）每个

6. （1）出生　　（2）生日　　　　（3）特别　　　　（4）因为
   （5）上课　　（6）参观　　　　（7）然后　　　　（8）请

7. 略。

3. 我有四门课
Wǒ yǒu sì mén kè
I Have Got Four Subjects

句型 | Sentence Patterns

21. 这学期我有四门课。
Zhè xuéqī wǒ yǒu sì mén kè.

I have got four subjects this semester.

22. 我每天有三个小时课。
Wǒ měi tiān yǒu sān gè xiǎoshí kè.

I have got three hours of class every day.

23. 上午有课，下午没课。
Shàngwǔ yǒu kè, xiàwǔ méi kè.

I have classes in the morning and none in the afternoon.

24. 我晚上经常去图书馆看书。
Wǒ wǎnshang jīngcháng qù túshūguǎn kàn shū.

I often go to the library at night for reading.

25. 我上电脑课了。
Wǒ shàng diànnǎo kè le.

I have attended the computer class.

3 我有四门课
I Have Got Four Subjects

26. 你中午在哪儿吃饭？
Nǐ zhōngwǔ zài nǎr chī fàn?
Where do you have lunch?

27. 中午我在学校餐厅吃饭。
Zhōngwǔ wǒ zài xuéxiào cāntīng chī fàn.
I have lunch in the school canteen.

28. 我最喜欢中国历史课。
Wǒ zuì xǐhuan Zhōngguó lìshǐ kè.
I like subject of Chinese history the most.

29. 我打算继续学习汉语。
Wǒ dǎsuan jìxù xuéxí Hànyǔ.
I plan to continue to study Chinese.

30. 我们快要放假了。
Wǒmen kuài yào fàng jià le.
The vacation is coming soon.

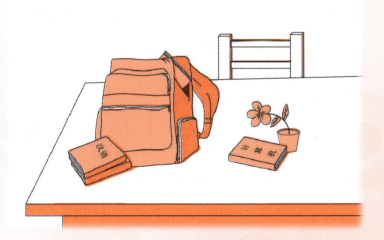

课文 | Text

(一)

男1: 这学期你有几门课?
Zhè xuéqī nǐ yǒu jǐ mén kè?
How many subjects have you got this semester?

男2: 我有四门课。
Wǒ yǒu sì mén kè.
I have got four subjects.

男1: 什么课?
Shénme kè?
What are they?

男2: 汉语、中国历史、中国文学和电脑课。
Hànyǔ、Zhōngguó lìshǐ、Zhōngguó wénxué hé diànnǎo kè.
Chinese, Chinese history, Chinese literature and computer.

男1: 你每天都有课吗?
Nǐ měi tiān dōu yǒu kè ma?
Do you have classes every day?

男2: 除了星期六和星期天,我每天都上课。
Chúle Xīngqīliù hé Xīngqītiān, wǒ měi tiān dōu shàng kè.
I have classes except on Saturday and Sunday.

3 我有四门课
I Have Got Four Subjects

男1: 上午上课还是下午上课?
Shàngwǔ shàng kè háishi xiàwǔ shàng kè?
Do you have classes in the morning or afternoon?

男2: 上午有课,下午没课。
Shàngwǔ yǒu kè, xiàwǔ méi kè.
I have classes in the morning, not in the afternoon.

男1: 下午你干什么?
Xiàwǔ nǐ gàn shénme?
What do you do in the afternoon?

男2: 我经常去图书馆看书。
Wǒ jīngcháng qù túshūguǎn kàn shū.
I often go to the library to read.

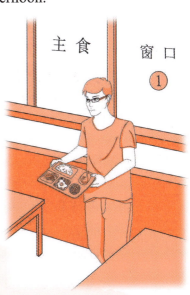

男1: 你中午在哪儿吃饭?
Nǐ zhōngwǔ zài nǎr chī fàn?
Where do you have lunch?

男2: 中午我在学校餐厅吃饭。
Zhōngwǔ wǒ zài xuéxiào cāntīng chī fàn.
I have lunch in the school canteen.

男1: 餐厅的饭怎么样?
Cāntīng de fàn zěnmeyàng?
How is the food in the canteen?

男2: 不错,很便宜。
Búcuò, hěn piányi.
Good enough and it is very cheap.

(二)

男: 你每天有几个小时课?
Nǐ měi tiān yǒu jǐ gè xiǎoshí kè?
How many hours of classes do you have every day?

女: 我每天有四个小时课。
Wǒ měi tiān yǒu sì gè xiǎoshí kè.
I have got four hours of classes every day.

男: 每天都有中文课吗?
Měi tiān dōu yǒu Zhōngwén kè ma?
Do you have Chinese lesson every day?

女: 是,每天都有一个小时中文课。
Shì, měi tiān dōu yǒu yí gè xiǎoshí Zhōngwén kè.
I have got one hour of Chinese lesson every day.

男: 你的中文老师是哪国人?
Nǐ de Zhōngwén lǎoshī shì nǎ guó rén?
Where does your Chinese teacher come from?

女: 是中国人。
Shì Zhōngguórén.
He is a Chinese.

男: 他的课有意思吗?
Tā de kè yǒu yìsi ma?
Is his class interesting?

3 我有四门课
I Have Got Four Subjects

女：一点儿意思也没有。
Yìdiǎnr yìsi yě méiyǒu.
It is not interesting at all.

男：什么课有意思？
Shénme kè yǒu yìsi?
What are the interesting classes?

女：电脑课最有意思。这学期我上电脑课了。
Diànnǎo kè zuì yǒu yìsi. Zhè xuéqī wǒ shàng diànnǎo kè le.
Computer class is most interesting. I attend computer class this semester.

（三）快放假了 The holiday is coming

这学期我有四门课：德语、中国历史、法国文学和电脑课。我的课都在上午，中午我在学校餐厅吃饭，下午和晚上我经常去图书馆看书。我最喜欢中国历史课。中国有几千年的历史，有很多有意思的事，我很想了解中国。现在学校快要放假了，我打算在假期里继续学习汉语，我想快点看懂中国历史书。

I have got four subjects this semester: German, Chinese history, French literature and Computer. All my classes are in the morning. I have lunch in the school canteen at the noon. I often go to the library to read in the afternoon and at night. I like Chinese history class the most. China has a history of several thousand years with a lot of interesting stories. I want very much to know about

China. Holiday is coming soon. I intend to continue to study Chinese in the holiday. I want to be able to read Chinese history book soon.

注释 | Annotation

1. **上午上课还是下午上课？Do you have classes in the morning or afternoon?**

    汉语中表示时间的名词有"早上、上午、中午、下午、晚上"等，它们可以在主语前，也可以在主语后。如：

    "早上、上午、中午、下午、晚上" are the five nouns indicating time in Chinese. They can be used both before and after the subject. For example:

    （1）我上午有课。

    I have classes in the morning.

    （2）上午我有课。

    In the morning, I have classes.

2. **下午没课。No classes in the afternoon.**

    "没"表示"没有"，口语中常用。

    "没 (no)" means "没有", usually used in colloquialism.

3 我有四门课
I Have Got Four Subjects

语法 | Grammar

1. 最

"最"用在形容词或某些动词前面,表示程度,意思是达到极点。如:

"最", used before adjectives and some verbs, is to indicate the maximum degree. For example:

(1) 最好的绿茶

the best green tea

(2) 电脑课最有意思。

The computer class is the most interesting.

(3) 我最喜欢流行音乐。

I like pop music the best.

2. 快……了,快要……了,要……了

是汉语中三个表示动作将要发生的句型,都表示动作很快要发生。如:

These are the three structures to express actions that will happen soon. For example:

(1) 快吃饭了。

The meal is to be ready soon.

(2) 快要开学了。

The school starts soon.

(3) 要上课了。

Lessons are going to start.

练习 | Exercises

1. 听录音，选择合适的回答：

Listen to the record and choose a proper answer:

（1）A. 我有四门课。
　　　B. 我每天都有课。

（2）A. 我中午在餐厅吃饭。
　　　B. 我去图书馆。

（3）A. 我每天有四个小时课。
　　　B. 我每天都有中文课。

（4）A. 汉语老师是中国人。
　　　B. 一点儿意思也没有。

2. 完成对话：

Complete the following dialogues:

（1）A：几点了？
　　　B：_____。
　　　A：我们几点有课？
　　　B：_____。
　　　A：走吧，要上课了。
　　　B：_____。

（2）A：今天星期几？
　　　B：_____。

3 我有四门课
I Have Got Four Subjects

　　A：我们有没有电脑课？
　　B：没有，_____。
　　A：我们有什么课？
　　B：_____。（中国历史、汉语）
(3) A：你每天都有课吗？
　　B：不，_____。
　　A：晚上你经常干什么？
　　B：_____。
　　A：还干什么？
　　B：_____。
(4) A：我们快要放假了吧？
　　B：是的，_____。
　　A：这学期你有几门课？
　　B：_____。
　　A：什么课最有意思？
　　B：_____。

3. 把下列词连成句子：

Join the following phrases into complete sentences:

(1) 在　餐厅　我　吃　每天　饭　都

_____

(2) 打算　我　学期　这　电脑　上　课

_____

(3) 经常　听　在　他　晚上　家　音乐

_____

(4) 汉语课 我 除了 喜欢 历史课 还
_____

(5) 上课 三个小时 每天 我 上午
_____

(6) 放假 我们 了 快要 学校
_____

(7) 了解 中国 他 想 非常
_____

(8) 一点儿 历史 课 也 意思 没有
_____

4. 选词填空：

Fill in the following blanks with the given words:

学期　不错　门　中国历史　喜欢　懂　有意思
便宜　作品　有的　了解　餐厅　历史　常常

我 (1)____ 学习汉语。这 (2)____ 我有四 (3)____ 课：汉语、(4)____、文学 (5)____ 和电脑课。我的课 (6)____ 在上午，有的在下午。中午我在 (7)____ 吃饭。餐厅的饭 (8)____，很 (9)____。晚上我 (10)____ 去图书馆。我的汉语课很 (11)____。中国有几千年的 (12)____，我想 (13)____ 中国，我要看 (14)____ 中文书。

5. 用下列词语描写一下你的学校生活：

Describe your campus life with the following words:

参考词语：早上　上午　中午　下午　晚上　经常　喜欢

3 我有四门课
I Have Got Four Subjects

生词 | New Words

1	门	mén	(量)	*measure word*	四门课 / four subjects 两门外语 two foreign languages 这个学期你有几门课？ How many subjects do you have this semester?
2	课	kè	(名)	class; lesson; subject	中国文学课 Chinese literature class 法国历史课 French history class 德语课 / German class
3	学期	xuéqī	(名)	semester; school term	这个学期 / this semester 上学期 / last semester 这个学期我有汉语课。 I have Chinese classes this semester.
4	小时	xiǎoshí	(名)	hour	一个小时 / one hour 每个小时 / each hour 我每天有四个小时课。 I have four hour of classes every day.
5	上午	shàngwǔ	(名)	morning	今天上午 / this morning 上午十点 / ten in the morning 我的课都在上午。 My classes are all in the morning.
6	图书馆	túshūguǎn	(名)	library	去图书馆 / go to the library 在图书馆看书 read in the library 你几点去图书馆？ When do you go to the library?
7	电脑	diànnǎo	(名)	computer	电脑课 / computer class 用（yòng, use）电脑 use a computer 你会修(xiū, repair)电脑吗？ Do you know how to repair a computer?

8	中午	zhōngwǔ	（名）	noon; midday	中午十二点 / 12 o'clock at noon 我中午不在家。 I'm not in at noon. 我每天中午都要休息一会儿。 I take a rest at noon every day.
9	吃	chī	（动）	to eat	吃橘子 / eat tangerines 吃面包 / eat bread 我最喜欢吃苹果。 The apple is my favorite.
10	饭	fàn	（名）	meals	吃饭 / have meals 我今天中午没吃饭。 I didn't have lunch today. 这儿的饭怎么样？ How's the food here?
11	学校	xuéxiào	（名）	school	在学校 / at school 星期六我不去学校。 I don't go to the school on Saturday. 我晚上在学校学习。 I study at school in the evening.
12	餐厅	cāntīng	（名）	canteen	学校餐厅 / school canteen 你经常去餐厅吗？ Do you often go to the canteen? 餐厅的饭怎么样？ How's the food in the canteen?
13	便宜	piányi	（形）	cheap	特别便宜 / very cheap 便宜极了 / so cheap 在餐厅吃饭很便宜。 It's very cheap to eat in the canteen.
14	快	kuài	（副）	soon	快上课了。 Class is beginning soon. 快吃饭了。 It's near the dining time now.

3 我有四门课
I Have Got Four Subjects

15	放假	fàng jià		to be on vacation	学校几月放假？ Which month will the school be on vacation? 我们快要放假了。 We are about to be on vacation. 我们公司放三天假。 Our company gives us a 3 day holiday.
16	继续	jìxù	（动） to continue	继续努力 / keep up 继续弹钢琴 continue to play the piano 我打算继续学习汉语。 I decide to continue my study of Chinese.

听力录音文本及参考答案

1. （1）这学期你有几门课？
   （2）你下午干什么？
   （3）你每天有几个小时课？
   （4）汉语课有意思吗？
   （1）A　（2）B　（3）A　（4）B

2. 略。

3. （1）我每天都在餐厅吃饭。
   （2）我这学期打算上电脑课。
   （3）他晚上经常在家听音乐。
   （4）除了汉语课，我还喜欢历史课。/ 除了历史课，我还喜欢汉语课。
   （5）我每天上午上三个小时课。
   （6）我们学校快要放假了。
   （7）他非常想了解中国。
   （8）历史课一点儿意思也没有。

4. （1）喜欢　（2）学期　（3）门　（4）中国历史　（5）作品
   （6）有的　（7）餐厅　（8）不错　（9）便宜　（10）常常
   （11）有意思　（12）历史　（13）了解　（14）懂

5. 略。

4 动物园在马路南边
Dòngwùyuán zài mǎlù nánbian

The Zoo Is on the Southern Side of the Road

句型 | Sentence Patterns

31. 请问，附近有没有公园？
Qǐngwèn, fùjìn yǒu méiyǒu gōngyuán?
Could you please tell me if there is any park nearby?

32. 附近只有动物园。
Fùjìn zhǐ yǒu dòngwùyuán.
There is only a zoo nearby.

33. 能告诉我怎么走吗？
Néng gàosu wǒ zěnme zǒu ma?
Would you please tell me how to get there?

34. 顺着这条马路一直往东（西）走。
Shùnzhe zhè tiáo mǎlù yìzhí wǎng dōng (xī) zǒu.
Along this road all the way to the east (west).

35. 动物园在马路南（北）边。
Dòngwùyuán zài mǎlù nán(běi)bian.
The zoo is on the southern (northern) side of the road.

4 动物园在马路南边

The Zoo Is on the Southern Side of the Road ▶

36. 对面是一个大商店。
Duìmiàn shì yí gè dà shāngdiàn.

There is a big department store in the opposite.

37. 有多远?
Yǒu duō yuǎn?

How far is it?

38. 不太远,走十分钟就到了。
Bú tài yuǎn, zǒu shí fēnzhōng jiù dào le.

Not too far. It takes only ten minutes' walk.

39. 动物园很好玩儿。
Dòngwùyuán hěn hǎowánr.

The zoo is very enjoyable.

40. 那儿有各种动物。
Nàr yǒu gè zhǒng dòngwù.

There are various kinds of animals.

课文 | Text

(一)

女： 请问附近有没有公园?
Qǐngwèn fùjìn yǒu méiyǒu gōngyuán?
Could you please tell me if there is any park nearby?

男： 附近只有动物园。
Fùjìn zhǐ yǒu dòngwùyuán.
There is only a zoo nearby.

女： 能告诉我怎么走吗?
Néng gàosu wǒ zěnme zǒu ma?
Would you please tell me how to get there?

男： 顺着这条马路一直往东走。
Shùnzhe zhè tiáo mǎlù yìzhí wǎng dōng zǒu.
Along this road and walk all the way to the east.

女： 一直往东吗?
Yìzhí wǎng dōng ma?
All the way to the east?

4 动物园在马路南边
The Zoo Is on the Southern Side of the Road

男: 一直往东走,然后再往右拐。
Yìzhí wǎng dōng zǒu, ránhòu zài wǎng yòu guǎi.
All the way to the east, then turn right.

女: 然后就到了?
Ránhòu jiù dào le?
Is it there then?

男: 是的,动物园在马路南边。
Shìde, dòngwùyuán zài mǎlù nánbian.
Yes, the zoo is on the southern side of the road.

女: 有多远?
Yǒu duō yuǎn?
How far is it?

男: 不太远,走十分钟就到了。
Bú tài yuǎn, zǒu shí fēnzhōng jiù dào le.
Not too far. It is only ten minutes' walk.

女: 谢谢!
Xièxie!
Thank you!

男: 不谢!
Bú xiè!
You are welcome!

(二)

女： 今天天气真好，不冷也不热。
Jīntiān tiānqì zhēn hǎo, bù lěng yě bú rè.

The weather today is really nice, neither cold nor hot.

男： 是啊，我们出去玩儿吧。
Shì a, wǒmen chūqu wánr ba.

Yes, let's go out and have some fun.

女： 好，去哪儿玩儿？
Hǎo, qù nǎr wánr?

All right. Where can we go?

男： 去动物园，怎么样？
Qù dòngwùyuán, zěnmeyàng?

How about to the zoo?

女： 动物园我去过了，去别的公园吧！
Dòngwùyuán wǒ qùguo le, qù biéde gōngyuán ba!

I have been there before. Let's go to some other parks.

男： 别的公园都太远了，还是动物园有意思。
Biéde gōngyuán dōu tài yuǎn le, háishì dòngwùyuán yǒu yìsi.

The other parks are too far away, and the zoo is more interesting.

女： 你喜欢去动物园？
Nǐ xǐhuan qù dòngwùyuán?

Do you like the zoo?

4 动物园在马路南边
The Zoo Is on the Southern Side of the Road

男： 动物园 很 好玩儿，有各 种 动物。我很 喜欢
Dòngwùyuán hěn hǎowánr, yǒu gè zhǒng dòngwù. Wǒ hěn xǐhuan
看 动物 吃 东西。
kàn dòngwù chī dōngxi.

The zoo is very interesting. It has got various kinds of animals. I like to watch animals feeding on food.

女： 好，那我们去 动物园。我 还 没 看过 熊猫 呢！
Hǎo, nà wǒmen qù dòngwùyuán. Wǒ hái méi kànguo xióngmāo ne!

All right. Let's go to the zoo then. I have never seen the panda yet!

(三) 动物园 The zoo

我们学校附近没有别的公园，只有动物园。动物园在我们学校的西边。顺着马路一直往西走就到了。动物园对面是一个大商店。星期六和星期天我们没有课，我和同学们经常一起去那儿玩儿。动物园不是很好玩儿，那儿只有各种动物。可是看动物吃东西是很有意思的事。

There are no parks near our school except the zoo. The zoo is to the west of our school. We would get there by walking all the way to the west along the road. There is a big store in the opposite. We have no classes on Saturday and Sunday. My classmates and I often go there to have some fun together. The zoo is not so interesting for it has only different kinds of animals. However, it is very interesting to watch animals feeding on food.

注释 | Annotation

1. 还是动物园有意思。 The zoo is more interesting.

　　"还是"在这里表示经过比较后的判断或选择。这个句子的意思是："和别的地方比，动物园更有意思。"

　　"还是", here, is to express the judgment or choice after comparison. The meaning of this sentence is "comparing to other places, the zoo is more interesting".

2. 熊猫　panda

　　中国的国宝级动物，主要生活在四川、陕西一带。喜欢吃竹子，十分可爱。

　　The panda, the animal of China's national treasure, living mainly in Sichuan and Shanxi province, liking to eat bamboo, is very lovely.

语法 | Grammar

1. 有、是、在

　　这三个动词都可以表示存在。用"有、是"表示存在时，主语往往是表示方位或地点的名词。用"在"表示存在时，主语经常是所叙述的人或事物。如：

4 动物园在马路南边
The Zoo Is on the Southern Side of the Road

These three verbs all express existence. "有" and "是" are usually used with subjects indicating location and direction. "在" is usually used with subjects indicating persons or objects. For example:

(1) 东边有一个图书馆。

    There is a library on the east side.

(2) 对面是一个公园。

    There is a park in the opposite.

(3) 商店在学校旁边。

    The store is beside the school.

(4) 老师在餐厅。

    The teacher is in the canteen.

2. 各种

"各"是一个代词，它常和量词"种"一起修饰名词。如："各" is a pronoun often used with the measure word "种" to modify nouns. For example:

(1) 各种书

    all kinds of books

(2) 各种动物

    all kinds of animals

(3) 各种商店

    all kinds of stores

练习 | Exercises

1. 听录音，选择合适的回答：

Listen to the record and choose a proper answer:

（1）A. 有一个。

　　　B. 我喜欢去公园。

（2）A. 对面是一个大商店。

　　　B. 顺着这条马路一直往东走。

（3）A. 有。

　　　B. 不太远，走十分钟就到。

（4）A. 附近没有动物园。

　　　B. 很好玩儿，那儿有各种动物。

2. 完成对话：

Complete the following dialogues:

（1）A：去银行怎么走？

　　　B：_____。

　　　A：有多远？

　　　B：_____。

　　　A：谢谢！

　　　B：_____。

（2）A：请问，附近有银行吗？

　　　B：有，_____。

4 动物园在马路南边

The Zoo Is on the Southern Side of the Road

A：能告诉我怎么走吗？

B：_____。（一直，商店）

A：商店在哪儿？

B：_____。

(3) A：你经常出去玩儿吗？

B：_____。

A：你经常去哪儿玩儿？

B：_____。

A：动物园好玩儿吗？

B：_____。（可是）

(4) A：_____？

B：我经常出去买东西。

A：_____？

B：我经常买牛奶、面包、橘子。

A：_____？

B：我和朋友一起去。

3. 选词填空：

Choose the right word to fill in the following blanks:

　　是　　有　　在

(1) 学校（　　）动物园对面。

(2) 银行旁边（　　）一个商店。

(3) 那儿（　　）很多动物。

(4) 飞机场（　　）东边。

(5) 商店的旁边（　　）动物园。

(6) 长城饭店（　　）马路左边。

(7) 动物园的对面（　　）一个大商店。

(8) 前面（　　）很多人。

4. 替换练习：

Substitution exercises:

(1) 附近有没有<u>公园</u>？

    商店

    银行

    饭店

    动物园

(2) <u>图书馆</u>有<u>各种书</u>。

 动物园　　动物

 那儿　　　面包

 老师家　　茶

 餐厅　　　啤酒

5. 选择合适的下句，使句子完整：

Choose a proper following sentence in the right column to complete the sentences of the left column:

(1) 附近没有公园，　　A. 有各种动物。

(2) 一直往东走，　　　B. 不冷也不热。

(3) 不太远，　　　　　C. 去别的公园吧！

4 动物园在马路南边
The Zoo Is on the Southern Side of the Road

（4）今天天气真好，　　D. 然后再往右拐。
（5）动物园我去过了，　　E. 只有动物园。
（6）动物园很好玩儿，　　F. 走十分钟就到了。

6. 用下列词语说一段话：

Make a speech with the following words:

题目：我喜欢/不喜欢动物园

参考词语：有　没有　好玩儿　可是

生词 | New Words

1	动物园	dòngwùyuán	（名）	zoo	去动物园 / go to the zoo 北京动物园 / Beijing Zoo 动物园在马路右边。 The zoo is on the right side of the road.
2	附近	fùjìn	（名）	nearby	在附近 / be nearby 附近有一个商店。 There's a shop nearby. 附近有银行吗？ Is there any bank nearby?
3	公园	gōngyuán	（名）	park	去公园 / go to the park 在公园 / in the park 我喜欢去公园。 I like going to park.
4	只	zhǐ	（副）	only	只有一个人 / only one person 只有一个单人间。 Only a single room is available. 我只喝绿茶。 I only drink green tea.

5	告诉	gàosu	（动）	to tell	告诉他 / tell him 他告诉我，动物园很好。 He tells me that the zoo is very good. 你不应该告诉他。 You shouldn't have told him.
6	顺着	shùnzhe	（介）	along	顺着马路走 walk along the road 先顺着这条路走，然后往右拐。 Walk along this road first, and then turn right.
7	条	tiáo	（量）	measure word	一条路 / a road 顺这条路一直走。 Walk straight along this road. 顺着这条路往前走。 Walk forth along this road.
8	东	dōng	（名）	east	东边 / east side 在东边 / on the east 银行在商店东边。 The bank is on the east of the shop.
9	西	xī	（名）	west	西边 / west side 在西边 / on the west 动物园在马路西边。 The zoo is on the west side of the road.
10	南	nán	（名）	south	南边 / southern side 在南边 / on the south 马路南边有一个银行。 There's a bank on the southern side of the road.
11	南边	nánbian	（名）	southern side	在南边 / on the south 马路南边有一个商店。 There's a shop on the southern side of the road. 商店在南边。 The shop is at the south.

4 动物园在马路南边
The Zoo Is on the Southern Side of the Road

12	北	běi	(名)	north	北边 / northern side 在北边 / on the north 马路北边有两个商店。 There're two shops on the northern side of the road.
13	北边	běibian	(名)	northern side	在北边 / on the north 顺着这条路往北边走。 Walk along this road to the north. 马路北边有一个公园。 There's a park on the northern side of the road.
14	对面	duìmiàn	(名)	opposite	在对面 / be opposite 银行在马路对面。 The bank is opposite to the road. 公园对面有一个商店。 There is a shop opposite to the park.
15	分钟	fēnzhōng	(名)	minute	三分钟 / 3 minutes 走二十分钟 / 20 minutes' walk 银行不远,走十五分钟就到了。 The bank is not far, only 15 minutes' walk.
16	好玩儿	hǎowánr	(形)	enjoyable; interesting; amusing; fun	很好玩儿 / very fun 不好玩儿 / not fun 动物园不好玩儿。 It's not fun at the zoo.
17	各	gè	(代)	various; different	各位 / everybody 各种 / all kinds of 动物园有各种动物。 All kinds of animals can be seen in the zoo.
18	动物	dòngwù	(名)	animal	动物园 / zoo 很多动物 / various animals 我喜欢看动物。 I like watching animals.

19	真	zhēn	（副）	really	真远 / really far 真贵 / really expensive 这个老师真有意思。 This teacher is really interesting.
20	西边	xībian	（名）	west side	在西边 / on the west 银行在西边。 The bank is at the west. 银行在马路西边。 The bank is on the west side of the road.
21	熊猫	xióngmāo		panda	我没有看过熊猫。 I've never seen a panda. 我喜欢看熊猫吃东西。 I like watching pandas eating.
22	东西	dōngxi	（名）	things	买东西 / buy things 吃东西 / eat things 我要去商店买东西。 I want to go to the shop to buy something.

听力录音文本及参考答案

1. （1）劳驾，附近有没有公园？
   （2）能告诉我怎么走吗？
   （3）有多远？
   （4）动物园好玩儿吗？
   （1）A　（2）B　（3）B　（4）B

2. 略。

3. （1）在　（2）有/是　（3）有　（4）在　（5）是
   （6）在　（7）是/有　（8）有

4. 略。

5. （1）E　（2）D　（3）F　（4）B　（5）C　（6）A

6. 略。

5. Wǒ mǎi qù Shànghǎi de huǒchēpiào
我买去上海的火车票
I Want to Buy a Train Ticket to Shanghai

句型 | Sentence Patterns

---

41. 你好，我买一张火车票。
Nǐhǎo, wǒ mǎi yì zhāng huǒchēpiào.
Hello, one ticket please.

42. 你买去哪儿的火车票？
Nǐ mǎi qù nǎr de huǒchēpiào?
Where is your destination?

43. 你买哪天的火车票？
Nǐ mǎi nǎ tiān de huǒchēpiào?
What is the date of the ticket you want?

44. 我买3月2号去上海的火车票。
Wǒ mǎi sānyuè èrhào qù Shànghǎi de huǒchēpiào.
I want to buy a train ticket to Shanghai on March 2nd.

45. 25号的票都卖完了。
Èrshíwǔ hào de piào dōu màiwán le.
Tickets for the 25th are all sold out.

46. 请你明天再来。
Qǐng nǐ míngtiān zài lái.

Please come again tomorrow.

47. 每张票六百五十二块。
Měi zhāng piào liùbǎi wǔshí'èr kuài.

It costs six hundred and fifty-two *yuan* for each ticket.

48. 到上海要五个小时。
Dào Shànghǎi yào wǔ gè xiǎoshí.

It takes five hours to get to Shanghai.

49. 我喜欢坐火车旅行。
Wǒ xǐhuan zuò huǒchē lǚxíng.

I like traveling by train.

50. 我喜欢坐在火车上看风景。
Wǒ xǐhuan zuò zài huǒchē shang kàn fēngjǐng.

I like enjoying scenery in the train.

5 我买去上海的火车票
I Want to Buy a Train Ticket to Shanghai

课文 | Text

(一)

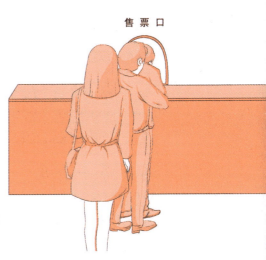

男：你好，我买 火车票。
Nǐhǎo, wǒ mǎi huǒchēpiào.
Hello, I want to buy a train ticket.

女：你买去哪儿的 火车票？
Nǐ mǎi qù nǎr de huǒchēpiào?
Where is your destination?

男：我买去 上海 的 火车票。
Wǒ mǎi qù Shànghǎi de huǒchēpiào.
I want a train ticket to Shanghai.

女：哪 天 的？
Nǎ tiān de?
On which day?

男：明天 的。
Míngtiān de.
Tomorrow.

女：对不起，明天的 火车票 都 卖完 了。
Duìbuqǐ, míngtiān de huǒchēpiào dōu màiwán le.
Sorry, the tickets for tomorrow are all sold out.

男：有 后天 的 票 吗？
Yǒu hòutiān de piào ma?
How about the day after tomorrow?

女：后天 的票 还有，你要几张？
Hòutiān de piào hái yǒu, nǐ yào jǐ zhāng?
There are still some for the day after tomorrow. How many do you want?

男：我要 两 张。
Wǒ yào liǎng zhāng.
I want two.

女：每 张 四百 五十二 块。
Měi zhāng sìbǎi wǔshí'èr kuài.
Four hundred and fifty-two Yuan for each.

男：请 等一会儿。
Qǐng děng yíhuìr.
A moment, please.

女：你不买了吗？
Nǐ bù mǎi le ma?
Do you still want them?

男：不，我要买，可是我的 钱不够。
Bù, wǒ yào mǎi, kěshì wǒ de qián bú gòu.
Yes, I want them, however, I do not have enough money.

女：那你 明天 再来吧。
Nà nǐ míngtiān zài lái ba.
Come again tomorrow then.

5 我买去上海的火车票
I Want to Buy a Train Ticket to Shanghai

(二)

男：劳驾，有到 上海 的 火车票 吗？
Láojià, yǒu dào Shànghǎi de huǒchēpiào ma?
Excuse me, is there any ticket to Shanghai?

女：有，你要哪一次的？
Yǒu, nǐ yào nǎ yí cì de?
Yes, which train do you want?

男：哪次车最快？
Nǎ cì chē zuì kuài?
Which train is the fastest?

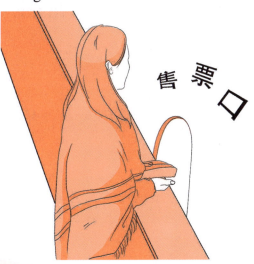

女：G 3次最 快。
G sān cì zuì kuài.
Train No.G3 is the fastest.

男：到 上海 要几个 小时？
Dào Shànghǎi yào jǐ gè xiǎoshí?
How long does it take to get to Shanghai?

女：大约 五个 小时就到了。
Dàyuē wǔ gè xiǎoshí jiù dào le.
It takes about five hours.

男：哪次车最舒服？
Nǎ cì chē zuì shūfu?
Which train is the most comfortable one?

女：也是 G 3次。
Yě shì G sān cì.
Train No.G3 too.

男：好，我要一张。
　　Hǎo, wǒ yào yì zhāng.
All right. I want one for that train.

（三）去上海旅行 To travel to Shanghai

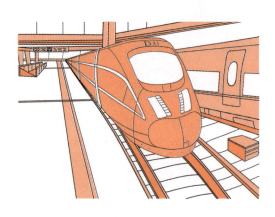

学校快放假了，大卫打算坐火车去上海旅行，因为他很喜欢坐火车，很喜欢坐在火车上看外面的风景。去上海的火车每天有很多次，他不知道哪次最好。他去问王红，王红告诉他，G3次车最好，因为G3次车最快，五个小时就到上海了。可是G3次车的车票比较贵，每张要四百五十二块。大卫喜欢快一点儿的车，他要坐G3次火车去上海。

　　The school vacation comes soon. David plans to travel to Shanghai by train, for he likes taking the train and enjoying scenery out of the window in the train. There are so many trains to Shanghai everyday that he does not know which is the best. He goes to ask Wang Hong and she tells him that Train No.G3 is the best because it is the fastest, getting to Shanghai in five hours. However, train tickets for Train No.G3 is relatively expensive, each ticket is four hundred and fifty-two Yuan. David likes faster trains, so he will go to Shanghai by Train No. G3.

5 我买去上海的火车票
I Want to Buy a Train Ticket to Shanghai

注释 | Annotation

1. 明天的火车票都卖完了。The tickets for toworrow are all sold out.

   "卖完"是一个结果补语式。"完"出现在"卖"后，补充说明"卖"的结果。类似的结构还有"吃完、说完、写完"。

   "卖完" is in the resultant complement mood. "完" is placed after "卖" to show the result of "卖". Other similar structures such as "吃完、说完、写完".

2. 劳驾　excuse me

   "劳驾"是汉语中非常常用的礼貌用语之一，用在句子开头。

   "劳驾", used at the beginning of a sentence, is a very common word to express politeness in Chinese.

3. 你要哪一次的？ Which train do you want?

   "次"可以表示火车的车次，如G3次。

   "次" could be used to identify the number of train, such as "G3次".

语法 | Grammar

1. 坐火车旅行

    这是一个连动词组，第二个动词性成分（旅行）表示第一个动作（坐火车）的目的。如：

    This is a phrase containing serial verbs in Chinese. The second verb (旅行) indicates the purpose of the first action (坐火车). For example:

    （1）去商店买东西

    　　to go to the store to buy things

    （2）去北京学汉语

    　　to go to Beijing to learn Chinese

2. 在火车上

    "在……上"中间加名词性成分后表示处所。如：

    Nouns are inserted between the structure "在……上" to indicate location. For example:

    （1）在书上

    　　in the book

    （2）在马路上

    　　on the road

    （3）在汉语课上

    　　during the Chinese class

5 我买去上海的火车票
I Want to Buy a Train Ticket to Shanghai

练习 | Exercises

1. **听录音，选择合适的回答：**

   Listen to the record and choose a proper answer:

   （1）A. 你买去哪儿的火车票？

   　　B. 我也要买火车票。

   （2）A. 我要两张。

   　　B. 后天的票没有了吗？

   （3）A. 有很多车都去上海。

   　　B. 大约五个小时就到了。

   （4）A. 我很喜欢。

   　　B. 去上海的火车每天都有很多次。

2. **完成对话：**

   Complete the following dialogues:

   （1）A：你好，买一张票。

   　　B：_____。

   　　A：去北京的。

   　　B：_____。

   　　A：明天的。

   　　B：_____。

   （2）A：你喜欢坐火车吗？

   　　B：_____。

A：为什么？
B：＿＿＿＿＿＿＿＿＿＿＿＿＿＿＿。
A：你经常坐火车旅行吗？
B：＿＿＿＿＿＿＿＿＿＿＿＿＿＿＿。

(3) A：你要买火车票吗？
B：＿＿＿＿＿＿＿＿＿＿＿＿＿＿＿。
A：哪一次的？
B：＿＿＿＿＿＿＿＿＿＿＿＿＿＿＿。
A：要几张？
B：＿＿＿＿＿＿＿＿＿＿＿＿＿＿＿。

(4) A：学校要放假了吧？
B：＿＿＿＿＿＿＿＿＿＿＿＿＿＿＿。
A：你打算去哪儿旅行？
B：＿＿＿＿＿＿＿＿＿＿＿＿＿＿＿。
A：坐火车去吗？
B：＿＿＿＿＿＿＿＿＿＿＿＿＿＿＿。

3. 翻译：

Translation:

(1) 早上　　上午　　中午　　下午　　晚上
(2) 今天　　明天　　后天
(3) 年　　月　　日　　星期
(4) 元　　角　　分
(5) 东　　西　　南　　北　　左　　右

（6）前边　　旁边　　对面
（7）那　　那儿　　哪　　哪儿

4. 连词造句：

Join the following words into complete sentences:

（1）火车票　明天　卖完了　的　都

_____

（2）两张　我　去　北京　要　火车票　的

_____

（3）喜欢　我　看　风景　坐在火车　外面的　上

_____

（4）北京　到上海　小时　五个　只要

_____

（5）放假了　快　王红　学校　打算　旅行　去

_____

5. 用下列词语续写：

Complete the passage with the following words:

我很（不）喜欢坐火车，……

参考词语：火车票　旅行　坐在火车上　外面的　风景
　　　　　舒服　快　贵

生词 | New Words

1	张	zhāng	（量）	measure word	一张票 / a ticket 一张登记表 / a piece of registration form 你好，我买一张票。 Hello, I'd like to buy a ticket.
2	火车	huǒchē	（名）	train	一列火车 / a train 火车快极了。/ The train is fast. 坐火车很舒服。 It's very comfortable on the train.
3	票	piào	（名）	ticket	车票 / (bus or train) ticket 火车票 / train ticket 我买一张去上海的火车票。 I want to buy a train ticket to Shanghai.
4	卖	mài	（动）	to sell	卖票 / sell tickets 卖完 / sell out 火车票卖完了。 Train tickets are sold out.
5	明天	míngtiān	（名）	tomorrow	明天是星期天。 It's Sunday tomorrow. 明天你有空吗？ Will you be free tomorrow? 我要一张明天的火车票。 I'd like a train ticket of tomorrow.
6	百	bǎi	（数）	hundred	一百 / 100 三百五十 / 350 一共一百三十二块。 Altogether 132 Yuan.
7	坐	zuò	（动）	to sit	坐出租车 / take a taxi 坐火车 / by train 坐火车比坐汽车舒服。 The train is more comfortable than the bus.

5 我买去上海的火车票
I Want to Buy a Train Ticket to Shanghai

8	旅行	lǚxíng	（动）	to travel	来中国旅行 / travel to China 我喜欢旅行。 / I love traveling. 他去德国旅行了。 He's gone to Germany to travel.
9	上	shàng		in; on	在火车上 / on the train 在火车上我休息不好。 I can't rest well on the train.
10	风景	fēngjǐng	（名）	scenery; view	风景很好 / nice scenery 看风景 / sightseeing 我喜欢坐在火车上看风景。 I enjoy sightseeing from the view on a train.
11	后天	hòutiān	（名）	the day after tomorrow	后天是几号？ What's the date the day after tomorrow? 后天就放假了。 We'll on vacation the day after tomorrow. 后天我们一起去拜访老师吧。 Let's visit our teacher the day after tomorrow.
12	够	gòu	（动）	enough	不够 / not enough 我的钱不够。 I didn't bring enough money. 快点儿吧，时间不够了。 Hurry up, it's running out of time.
13	劳驾	láojià	（动）	excuse me	劳驾,银行在哪儿？ Excuse me, where's the bank? 劳驾,去美术馆怎么走？ Excuse me, how can I get to the art museum? 劳驾,我买一张票。 Excuse me, I'd like to buy a ticket.

| 14 | 次 | cì | （量） measure word | 哪次车最快？
Which train is the fastest?
G3次车最舒服。
G3 train is the most comfortable one.
我要坐G4次车去北京。
I will go to Beijing by Train No. G4. |

专有名词：

Proper noun:

| 上海 | Shànghǎi | name of a city |

听力录音文本及参考答案

1. （1）你好，我买火车票。
   （2）明天的票卖完了，有后天的。
   （3）请问，到上海要几个小时？
   （4）你喜欢坐火车吗？
   （1）A　（2）A　（3）B　（4）A

2. 略。

3. 略。

4. （1）明天的火车票都卖完了。
   （2）我要两张去北京的火车票。
   （3）我喜欢坐在火车上看外面的风景。
   （4）北京到上海只要五个小时。
   （5）学校快放假了，王红打算去旅行。

5. 略。

6 中餐厅在一楼
Zhōngcāntīng zài yī lóu
The Chinese Restaurant Is on the First Floor

句型 | Sentence Patterns

51. 中餐厅在一楼。
Zhōngcāntīng zài yī lóu.

The Chinese restaurant is on the first floor.

52. 西餐厅在二楼。
Xīcāntīng zài èr lóu.

The western restaurant is on the second floor.

53. 这儿的西餐怎么样?
Zhèr de xīcān zěnmeyàng?

How is the western food here?

54. 法国牛排和意大利面都很有名。
Fǎguó niúpái hé Yìdàlìmiàn dōu hěn yǒumíng.

Both the French beef chop and Italian spaghetti are very well-known.

55. 房间 里有 空调 和电视。
Fángjiān li yǒu kōngtiáo hé diànshì.

There are air-conditioner and television in the room.

56. 房间 里可以打国际电话。
Fángjiān li kěyǐ dǎ guójì diànhuà.

International calls can be made in the room.

57. 房间 里有洗衣服的口袋。
Fángjiān li yǒu xǐ yīfu de kǒudai.

Laundry bags are available in the room.

58. 每 天 都可以洗衣服。
Měi tiān dōu kěyǐ xǐ yīfu.

Laundry service is available every day.

59. 饭店 里住着 各 国 客人。
Fàndiàn li zhùzhe gè guó kèrén.

The hotel accommodates guests from all over the world.

60. 一边喝咖啡，一边 听音乐。
Yìbiān hē kāfēi, yìbiān tīng yīnyuè.

Drinking coffee while enjoying the music.

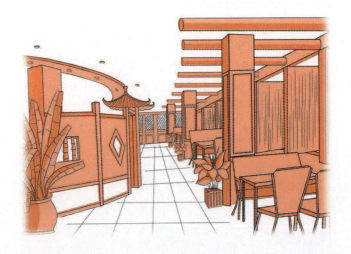

6 中餐厅在一楼
The Chinese Restaurant Is on the First Floor

课文 | Text

(一)

男： 劳驾，我要一间双人房间。
Láojià, wǒ yào yì jiān shuāngrén fángjiān.
Excuse me, I want a double room.

女： 对不起，双人房间都住满了，您要单人房间吧。
Duìbuqǐ, shuāngrén fángjiān dōu zhùmǎn le, nín yào dānrén fángjiān ba.
Sorry, double rooms are fully booked. Please take a single room.

男： 单人房间里有空调和电视吗？
Dānrén fángjiān li yǒu kōngtiáo hé diànshì ma?
Are there air-conditioner and television in the single room?

女： 有，有空调，也有电视，还有冰箱。
Yǒu, yǒu kōngtiáo, yě yǒu diànshì, hái yǒu bīngxiāng.
Yes, there are air-conditioner, television and refrigerator。

男： 在房间里可以打国际电话吗？
Zài fángjiān li kěyǐ dǎ guójì diànhuà ma?
Can I make international calls in the room?

女：可以。
Kěyǐ.
Yes.

男：在哪儿洗衣服？
Zài nǎr xǐ yīfu?
Where can I get the laundry service?

女：房间里有洗衣服的口袋，每天都可以洗。
Fángjiān li yǒu xǐ yīfu de kǒudai, měi tiān dōu kěyǐ xǐ.
There are laundry bags in the room. The laundry service is available every day.

男：单人房间多少钱一天？
Dānrén fángjiān duōshao qián yì tiān?
How much is a single room per day?

女：每天四百二十元。
Měi tiān sìbǎi èrshí yuán.
It costs four hundred and twenty *yuan* every day.

男：好，我要一间。
Hǎo, wǒ yào yì jiān.
All right, I take one.

女：请跟她走，您的房间在五楼。
Qǐng gēn tā zǒu, nín de fángjiān zài wǔ lóu.
Please follow her. Your room is on the fifth floor.

男：谢谢！
Xièxie!
Thank you!

6 中餐厅在一楼
The Chinese Restaurant Is on the First Floor

(二)

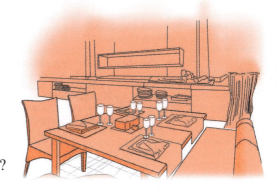

男：请问，餐厅在哪儿？
Qǐngwèn, cāntīng zài nǎr?

May I ask where the restaurant is?

女：中餐厅还是西餐厅？
Zhōngcāntīng háishi xīcāntīng?

Is it a Chinese or western restaurant?

男：中餐厅。
Zhōngcāntīng.

Chinese restaurant.

女：中餐厅在一楼。
Zhōngcāntīng zài yī lóu.

The Chinese restaurant is on the first floor.

男：这儿的西餐怎么样？
Zhèr de xīcān zěnmeyàng?

How is the western restaurant here?

女：很不错，法国牛排和意大利面都很有名。
Hěn búcuò, Fǎguó niúpái hé Yìdàlìmiàn dōu hěn yǒumíng.

Very good, both the French beef chop and Italian spaghetti are very well-known.

男：我要去试试，我很喜欢意大利面。
Wǒ yào qù shìshi, wǒ hěn xǐhuan Yìdàlìmiàn.

I want to try. I like Italian spaghetti very much.

女：西餐厅在二楼。
Xīcāntīng zài èr lóu.

The western restaurant is on the second floor.

（三）北京饭店 Beijing Hotel

北京饭店是一个有名的饭店。饭店里住着各国客人，日本人、英国人、德国人、美国人、法国人、意大利人……哪国人都有。饭店里有中餐厅，也有西餐厅。中餐厅很不错，西餐厅也很好。在西餐厅，你可以吃到法国牛排和意大利面。在饭店的二楼还有一个咖啡厅，在那儿喝咖啡很舒服，因为你可以一边喝咖啡，一边听音乐，那是一种很好的享受。

Beijing Hotel is a famous hotel. It accommodates guests from various countries: Japanese, English, German, American, French, Italian..., guests from all over the world. There are both Chinese and western restaurants in the hotel. The Chinese restaurant is very good, and so is the western restaurant where you can eat French beef chop and Italian spaghetti. There is a cafe on the second floor. It is comfortable to drink coffee there because you can drink coffee while listening to music. It is a good enjoyment.

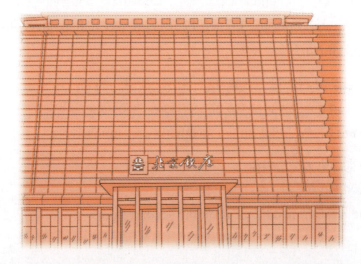

6 中餐厅在一楼
The Chinese Restaurant Is on the First Floor

注释 | Annotation

1. 哪国人都有。Guests from all over the world.

意思是"各个国家的人都有"。"哪"在这里是任指，表示"任何一个"。

This sentence means that "there are people from every country". "哪", here, is used as a general reference which means "anyone".

2. 那是一种很好的享受。It is a good enjoyment.

"那"用在句首，指代前边提到的内容。在本课中，"那"代替的是"在咖啡厅一边喝咖啡，一边听音乐"。

"那", used at the beginning of a sentence, is to refer to the content mentioned above. In this text, what "那" substitutes for is "drink coffee as while as listening to music in the cafe".

语法 | Grammar

1. 房间里

"名词+里"表示处所，常做主语或宾语。如：

"Noun+里" expresses locality, often used as subjects or objects. For example:

(1) 房间里有很多人。

There are many people in the room.

(2) 我的钥匙在车里。

My key is in the car.

2. 着

"动词 + 着"表示动作的持续。"着"常和"正"一起用，构成"正 + 动词 + 着 + 宾语"式。如：

"Verb + 着" indicates the action is still going on. "着" is often used together with "正" to form the pattern "正 + verb + 着 + object". For example:

(1) 他正吃着饭。

He is eating.

(2) 外面正刮着大风。

It is blowing strong wind outside.

3. 一边……一边……

表示两个动作同时发生。如：

This structure indicates that two actions take place at the same time. For example:

(1) 一边吃饭，一边听音乐。

Eating while listening to music.

(2) 一边看电视，一边做练习。

Watching television while doing the exercises.

6 中餐厅在一楼
The Chinese Restaurant Is on the First Floor

练习 | Exercises

1. 听句子，判断句子对错：

Listen to the record and judge whether the statements are correct or not:

(1) 中餐厅不在二楼。　☐
(2) 房间里没有空调。　☐
(3) 单人房间一天二百四十元。　☐
(4) 我住在五楼。　☐
(5) 饭店里都是美国人。　☐

2. 连线：

Matching:

(1) 有名的　　　　面
(2) 意大利　　　　房间
(3) 各国　　　　　饭店
(4) 双人　　　　　客人

3. 用"一边……一边……"把下列词组连成句子：

Use "一边……一边……" to join the following phrases into sentences:

(1) 看书　　　　听音乐
(2) 喝茶　　　　看电视
(3) 喝咖啡　　　看书

（4）看风景　　　听音乐
（5）吃饭　　　　打电话
（6）洗衣服　　　学习生词

4. 用"××里"回答问题：

Answer the following questions with "××里"：

（1）房间里有什么人？
（2）饭店里住着什么人？
（3）这个商店里卖什么？
（4）西餐厅里有什么？
（5）图书馆里有什么？
（6）冰箱里有什么？

5. 用指定词回答问题：

Answer the following questions with the given words:

（1）你去干什么？（打电话）
（2）晚上你想吃什么？（牛排）
（3）西餐厅在哪儿？（没有）
（4）面条怎么样？（不喜欢）
（5）我的房间在几楼？（十）

6 中餐厅在一楼
The Chinese Restaurant Is on the First Floor

6. 用下列词语介绍一个你喜欢的饭店（或饭馆）：

Introduce one of your favorite hotels (or restaurants) with the following words:

参考词语：有名　有……，有……，还有……　不错
　　　　　很好　一边……一边……　享受

生词 | New Words

1	中餐厅	zhōngcāntīng	（名）	Chinese restaurant	中餐厅在哪儿？ Where's the Chinese restaurant? 这是中餐厅。 Here's the Chinese restaurant. 中餐厅在东边。 The Chinese restaurant is at the east.
2	楼	lóu	（名）	floor	一楼 / 1st floor 三楼 / 3rd floor 中餐厅在二楼。 The Chinese restaurant is on the 2nd floor.
3	西餐厅	xīcāntīng	（名）	western restaurant	西餐厅在哪儿？ Where's the western restaurant? 这是西餐厅。 Here's the western restaurant. 西餐厅在一楼。 The western restaurant is on the 1st floor.

4	这儿	zhèr	（代）	here	这儿有三个公园。 Here're three parks. 老师在这儿。 The teacher's here. 这儿是动物园。 Here's the zoo.
5	牛排	niúpái	（名）	beef chop	法国牛排 / French beef chop 吃牛排 / eat beef chop 我喜欢吃牛排。 I like eating beef chop.
6	面	miàn	（名）	spaghetti; noodle	意大利面 / spaghetti 吃面 / eat noodles 这儿的面很有名。 Noodles here are very famous.
7	里	lǐ	（名）	in	公园里 / in the park 餐厅里 / in the restaurant 动物园里有各种动物。 There're various animals in the zoo.
8	空调	kōngtiáo	（名）	air-conditioner	买空调 buy an air-conditioner 这里有空调吗？ Do you have air-conditioners here? 我喜欢有空调的房间。 I like rooms with air-conditioner.
9	电视	diànshì	（名）	television	看电视 / watch TV 买电视 / buy a television 房间里有电视，也有空调。 There's an air-conditioner as well as a television in the room.
10	打	dǎ	（动）	to make (a call)	打电话 / make a call 给老师打电话 make a call to one's teacher 他正在给朋友打电话。 He's calling his friend.

6 中餐厅在一楼
The Chinese Restaurant Is on the First Floor

11	国际	guójì	（名）	international	国际电话 / international call 打国际电话 make international calls 打国际电话很贵。 International calls are expensive.
12	电话	diànhuà	（名）	telephone	打电话 / phone 打国际电话 make international calls 他正在给朋友打电话。 He's calling his friend.
13	洗	xǐ	（动）	to wash	洗衣服 / wash clothes 洗手(shǒu, hand) wash hands 我一般星期六洗衣服。 I usually wash my clothes on Saturday.
14	衣服	yīfu	（名）	clothes; dress	洗衣服 / wash clothes 一件衣服 / a dress 你的衣服真漂亮。 Your dress is so beautiful.
15	口袋	kǒudai	（名）	pocket; bag	一个口袋 / a pocket 请给我一个口袋。 Please give me a pocket. 房间里有洗衣服口袋。 Laundry bags are available in the room.
16	着	zhe	（助）	*particle*	饭店里住着各国客人。 There are guests from all countries in this hotel. 他正吃着东西。 He is eating something. 我正看着电视。 I am watching TV.

17	一边	yìbiān	（副）	at the same time	一边吃东西，一边看书。 Eating while reading a book. 一边看电视，一边做练习。 Watching TV while doing exercises. 我喜欢一边吃东西，一边看电视。 I like eating something while watching TV.
18	冰箱	bīngxiāng	（名）	refrigerator	一个冰箱 / a refrigerator 房间里有冰箱。 There's a refrigerator in the room. 我要买一个冰箱。 I want to buy a refrigerator.

专有名词：

Proper nouns:

1	意大利	Yìdàlì	Italy
2	日本人	Rìběnrén	Japanese
3	法国人	Fǎguórén	French
4	意大利人	Yìdàlìrén	Italian

听力录音文本及参考答案

1. （1）中餐厅在一楼。
   （2）房间里除了空调，还有电视。
   （3）单人房间一天四百二十元。
   （4）我的房间在五楼。
   （5）饭店里哪国人都有。
   （1）√　（2）×　（3）×　（4）√　（5）×
2. （1）有名的饭店
   （2）意大利面

6 中餐厅在一楼
The Chinese Restaurant Is on the First Floor

（3）各国客人

（4）双人房间

3. 略。
4. 略。
5. 略。
6. 略。

7 Nǐ de jiā zhēn piàoliang
你的家真漂亮
Your House Is Really Beautiful

句型 | Sentence Patterns

61. 欢迎你们到我家来玩儿。
Huānyín nǐmen dào wǒ jiā lái wánr.
You are welcome to visit my home.

62. 这些水果送给你。
Zhèxiē shuǐguǒ sònggěi nǐ.
These fruits are for you.

63. 你的家真漂亮。
Nǐ de jiā zhēn piàoliang.
Your house is really pretty.

64. 你的家又漂亮又舒服。
Nǐ de jiā yòu piàoliang yòu shūfu.
Your house is pretty and comfortable as well.

65. 我一定经常来。
Wǒ yídìng jīngcháng lái.
I would surely come back for visits.

7 你的家真漂亮
Your House Is Really Beautiful

66. 请 坐，喝点儿 什么？
Qǐng zuò, hēdiǎnr shénme?

Please take a seat. What would you like to drink?

67. 随便，什么 都 行。
Suíbiàn, shénme dōu xíng.

It is all right. Anything would do.

68. 我 饱 了，不 能 再 吃 了。
Wǒ bǎo le, bù néng zài chī le.

I am full and can eat no more.

69. 时间 不 早 了，我 该 走 了。
Shíjiān bù zǎo le, wǒ gāi zǒu le.

It's late. I have to go.

70. 欢迎 你 经常 来 玩儿。
Huānyíng nǐ jīngcháng lái wánr.

You are welcome back for visits.

课文 | Text

(一) (到朋友家做客 To be guest at a friend's home)

女: 欢迎 你们到 我家来玩儿。
Huānyíng nǐmen dào wǒ jiā lái wánr.
Welcome to my home.

男: 谢谢！这些水果 和这 瓶酒 送给你。
Xièxie! Zhèxiē shuǐguǒ hé zhè píng jiǔ sònggěi nǐ.
Thank you! These fruits and this bottle of wine are for you.

女: 你太客气了！
Nǐ tài kèqi le!
Thank you!

男: 你的家真 漂亮！
Nǐ de jiā zhēn piàoliang!
Your house is really pretty!

女: 是吗？谢谢！
Shì ma? xièxie!
Is it? Thank you!

男: 是的，你的家又 漂亮又 舒服。
Shìde, nǐ de jiā yòu piàoliang yòu shūfu.
Yes, your house is pretty and comfortable as well.

女: 欢迎 你 经常来 玩儿。
Huānyíng nǐ jīngcháng lái wánr.
You are welcome to come back.

7 你的家真漂亮
Your House Is Really Beautiful

男： 我一定经常来。
Wǒ yídìng jīngcháng lái.
I would surely come back for visits.

女： 请坐，喝点儿什么？
Qǐng zuò, hēdiǎnr shénme?
Please take a seat. What would you like to drink?

男： 随便，什么都行。
Suíbiàn, shénme dōu xíng.
It is all right. Anything would do.

女： 喝一杯茶吧！
Hē yì bēi chá ba!
Have a cup of tea then!

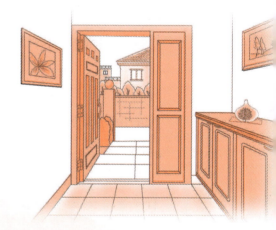

男： 好！
Hǎo!
All right!

（二）（在朋友家吃饭 Dining at a friend's home）

女： 你喜欢吃饺子吗？
Nǐ xǐhuan chī jiǎozi ma?
Do you like dumplings?

男： 很喜欢吃，中国饭里，我最喜欢吃饺子。
Hěn xǐhuan chī, Zhōngguó fàn li, wǒ zuì xǐhuan chī jiǎozi.
I like it very much. Of all Chinese food, I like dumplings the most.

女：那你多吃一点儿。
Nà nǐ duō chī yìdiǎnr.

You can eat more.

男：我已经吃了很多了。
Wǒ yǐjīng chī le hěn duō le.

I have already eaten a lot.

女：再吃点儿别的。
Zài chīdiǎnr biéde.

Please take something else.

男：我饱了,不能再吃了。
Wǒ bǎo le, bù néng zài chī le.

I am full and can eat nothing more.

女：吃点儿 水果吧,橘子又大又甜。
Chīdiǎnr shuǐguǒ ba, júzi yòu dà yòu tián.

Try some fruits then. The mandarin oranges are large and sweet.

男：好,我吃一个。
Hǎo, wǒ chī yí gè.

OK, I eat one.

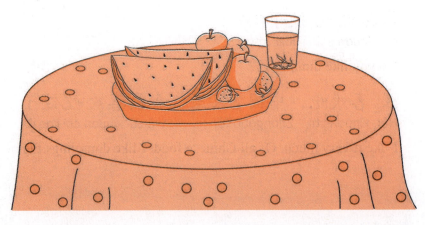

7 你的家真漂亮
Your House Is Really Beautiful

（三）在朋友家 At a friend's home

今天是星期天，天气特别好，不冷也不热。下午我和大卫一起去朋友家玩儿。朋友家在动物园附近，不太远，我们走了一会儿就到了。我们在朋友家玩儿得很高兴。我们一起喝茶，一起弹钢琴，一起听音乐。大约七点钟，我们开始吃晚饭。我们一边喝啤酒，一边吃饺子。饺子特别香，真好吃。然后我们又吃了水果。晚上我们还看了特别有意思的电视。十点了，我对朋友说："时间不早了，我们该走了。"朋友说："欢迎你们下次再来玩儿。"

It is Sunday today. The weather is particularly good, neither cold nor hot. David and I go together to visit a friend. His home is near the zoo, not too far away. It took only a while to walk there. We had a good time at our friend's house. We drank tea, played the piano and listened to music together. The dinner began around seven o'clock. We drank beer while eating dumplings. The dumplings are tasty, really delicious. Later we had some fruits. In the evening we watched some particularly interesting TV programs. When it was ten o'clock, I said to my friend, "It is late already, we have to go." Our friend said, "You are welcome to come back some day."

注释 | Annotation

1. 该走了。I have to go.

   "该"意思是"应该",口语中常用。

   "该" means "应该". It's commonly used in colloquial Chinese.

2. 欢迎你们下次再来玩儿。You are welcome to come back some day.

   "下次",意思是"下一次","次"在这里是量词。

   "下次" means the next time ("下一次"). "次" is a measure word in this case.

语法 | Grammar

1. 又……又……

   表示几种情况同时存在,"又"后经常加形容词。如:
   This structure indicates the coexistence of several situations. "又" is often followed by adjectives. For example:

   (1) 又大又甜

   　　big and sweet as well

7 你的家真漂亮
Your House Is Really Beautiful

(2) 又好又便宜

　　good (quality) and cheap as well

2. 多吃一点儿

　　"多"常加在动词前做状语，动词后边常用"一点儿""一些""一会儿""几个"。如：

　　"多" is often used before verbs as adverbial modifier. The verbs are often followed by phrases of "一点儿""一些""一会儿""几个". For example:

(1) 多买一些

　　to buy some more

(2) 多等一会儿

　　to wait for another while

(3) 多吃几个

　　to eat a few more

3. 已经

　　是用来表示动作完成的副词，常和"了"一起用。

　　It's an adverb used to express the completion of an action often used with "了".

(1) 已经十点了。

　　It's ten already.

(2) 我已经吃了很多了。

　　I have eaten a lot.

练习 | Exercises

1. 听录音，选择合适的回答：

Listen to the record and choose a proper answer:

(1) A. 谢谢，我很高兴。
　　B. 我不喜欢玩儿。
　　C. 我们该走了。

(2) A. 没关系。
　　B. 欢迎，欢迎。
　　C. 你太客气了。

(3) A. 饺子是中国饭。
　　B. 我很喜欢吃。
　　C. 我吃了大约十个。

(4) A. 我再吃点儿。
　　B. 我已经吃了很多了。
　　C. 橘子又大又甜。

(5) A. 是吗？谢谢。
　　B. 你太客气了，再见。
　　C. 欢迎你们经常来玩儿。

7 你的家真漂亮
Your House Is Really Beautiful

2. 用"又……又……"把下列词组成句子:

Use "又……又……" to join the following words into complete sentences:

(1) 贵　　　　不舒服
(2) 便宜　　　好
(3) 大　　　　甜
(4) 漂亮　　　舒服
(5) 快　　　　好

3. 替换练习:

Substitution exercises:

(1) 你的<u>身体</u>真<u>好</u>。
　　　家　　舒服
　　　书　　多
　　　汉语　好

(2) <u>他</u>已经<u>走了</u>。
　　　我　　起床
　　　老师　开始工作
　　　学校　放假

4. 选词填空:

Fill in the following blanks with the given phrases:

　　多买一些　多等一会儿　多吃一点儿　多玩儿一会儿

(1) 今天的饺子很好吃,你(　　　　)。

(2) 你（　　），他就要来了。
(3) 天气真好，我们（　　）吧！
(4) 这种橘子很好吃，你（　　）吧！

5. 把下面的句子按顺序排列：

   Arrange the following sentences in right order:
   (1) 下午我和朋友一起到老师家玩儿。
   (2) 我们送给老师一瓶酒和一些水果。
   (3) 今天的天气特别好，不冷也不热。
   (4) 老师的家很漂亮，又大又舒服。
   (5) 我们在老师家玩儿得很高兴。
   (6) 老师请我们喝茶，还请我们吃饺子。

6. 用下列词语写一段话：

   Write a passage with the following words:
   题目：我的家
   参考词语：又……又……　漂亮　舒服　附近

生词 | New Words

1	漂亮	piàoliang	（形）	pretty	漂亮的风景 / nice scenery 北京饭店很漂亮。 Beijing Hotel is beautiful. 你的家真漂亮。 Your house is really beautiful.

7 你的家真漂亮
Your House Is Really Beautiful

2	玩	wán	（动）	to play	到他家玩 / go play at his home 去动物园玩 / go play in the zoo 欢迎你到我家来玩。 Welcome to my house to play.
3	些	xiē	（量）	measure word	一些 / some 一些苹果 / some apples 这些书我都看过。 I've seen all these books.
4	水果	shuǐguǒ	（名）	fruits	这些水果 / these fruits 几种水果 / several kinds of fruits 你喜欢吃哪种水果？ Which kind of fruit do you prefer?
5	送	sòng	（动）	to send; to give	送礼物(lǐwù, gift) give presents. 送你一瓶酒。 Here's a bottle of wine for you. 这是送你的礼物。 This is my gift for you.
6	给	gěi	（动）	to give	给你 / give it to you 给你这本书 / give you this book 这些水果送给你。 These fruits are for you.
7	又	yòu	（副）	as well; also	你家又漂亮又舒服。 Your home is comfortable as well as beautiful. 餐厅卖的咖啡又好喝又便宜。 Coffee in the canteen tastes very good, and also very cheap. 上海又大又漂亮。 Shanghai is big as well as beautiful.
8	一定	yídìng	（副）	surely; definitely	我一定要去。 / I'll surely go. 我一定经常来。 I'll surely come at every turn. 我一定努力学习汉语。 I must learn Chinese well.

9	随便	suíbiàn	（动）	(colloquial) as you like	请随便吧,别客气。 Help yourselves. Be at home. 你随便,想吃什么就吃什么。 You can eat what you want. Be at home.
10	饱	bǎo	（形）	fully fed	吃饱 / be full 我饱了。 / I'm full. 我吃饱了,不能吃了。 I'm so full that I can't eat more.
11	瓶	píng	（量）	measure word	一瓶啤酒 / a bottle of beer 一瓶可乐（kělè,Cola） a bottle of Cola 你能喝几瓶啤酒? How many bottles of beer can you drink?
12	酒	jiǔ	（名）	alcohol	白酒 / wine 红酒 / red wine 他特别爱喝酒。 He's an alcoholic.
13	饺子	jiǎozi	（名）	dumpling	吃饺子 / eat dumplings 几个饺子 / several dumplings 你会包(bāo,make)饺子吗? Do you know how to make Chinese dumplings?
14	已经	yǐjīng	（副）	already	已经走了 / already gone 已经吃过了 / already ate 我已经到北京了。 I've already been in Beijing.

听力录音文本及参考答案

1. (1) 欢迎你到我家来玩儿。
　(2) 这些水果送给你。
　(3) 你喜欢吃饺子吗?
　(4) 你多吃点儿橘子。
　(5) 时间不早了,我们该走了。
　(1) A　(2) C　(3) B　(4) B　(5) C

7 你的家真漂亮
Your House Is Really Beautiful

2. 略。
3. 略。
4. （1）多吃一点儿　（2）多等一会儿　（3）多玩儿一会儿　（4）多买一些
5. （3）—（1）—（4）—（2）—（6）—（5）
6. 略。

8 这件衣服很漂亮
Zhè jiàn yīfu hěn piàoliang
This Dress Is Very Pretty

句型 | Sentence Patterns

71. 这件衣服很漂亮。
Zhè jiàn yīfu hěn piàoliang.
This dress is very pretty.

72. 绿颜色对你很合适。
Lǜ yánsè duì nǐ hěn héshì.
Green is your color.

73. 我不喜欢红颜色的。
Wǒ bù xǐhuan hóng yánsè de.
I do not like dresses in red color.

74. 这件是小号的。
Zhè jiàn shì xiǎo hào de.
This piece is small-sized.

75. 我应该穿中号的。
Wǒ yīnggāi chuān zhōng hào de.
My size is medium.

8 这件衣服很漂亮
This Dress Is Very Pretty

76. 这条裙子的颜色、样子都好看。
Zhè tiáo qúnzi de yánsè, yàngzi dōu hǎokàn.

Both the color and pattern of this skirt are nice.

77. 这条裙子太短了。
Zhè tiáo qúnzi tài duǎn le.

This skirt is too short.

78. 我喜欢穿长一点儿的裙子。
Wǒ xǐhuan chuān cháng yìdiǎnr de qúnzi.

I would like the skirt to be a little longer.

79. 这条比那条长。
Zhè tiáo bǐ nà tiáo cháng.

This one is longer than that one.

80. 有的太大,有的太小。
Yǒude tài dà, yǒude tài xiǎo.

Some are too big, and some are too small.

课文 | Text

(一)

女1: 王红,这件衣服怎么样?
Wáng Hóng, zhè jiàn yīfu zěnmeyàng?
Wang Hong, how about this dress?

女2: 不错,多少钱?
Búcuò, duōshao qián?
Good, how much is it?

女1: 八十。
Bāshí.
Eighty Yuan.

女2: 又便宜又漂亮,你买一件吧!
Yòu piányi yòu piàoliang, nǐ mǎi yí jiàn ba!
It's cheap and pretty. Why not buy one?

女1: 颜色怎么样?是绿色的。
Yánsè zěnmeyàng? Shì lǜsè de.
How about the color? It is green.

女2: 绿颜色对你很合适。
Lǜ yánsè duì nǐ hěn héshì.
Green is your color.

女1: 是吗?我试试。
Shì ma? Wǒ shìshi.
Is it? I would like to have a try.

8 这件衣服很漂亮
This Dress Is Very Pretty

女2： 真 漂亮，买吧！
Zhēn piàoliang, mǎi ba!

It is really pretty! Take it!

女1： 这件是小号的，我穿有点儿小。我应该穿中号的。
Zhè jiàn shì xiǎo hào de, wǒ chuān yǒudiǎnr xiǎo. Wǒ yīnggāi chuān zhōng hào de.

This one is the small size, a little bit too small for me. My size is medium.

女2： 你试试中号的，中号的一定合适。
Nǐ shìshi zhōng hào de, zhōng hào de yídìng héshì.

Then please try the medium size. It must fit you.

女1： 中号的只有红颜色的，我不喜欢。
Zhōng hào de zhǐ yǒu hóng yánsè de, wǒ bù xǐhuan.

Medium size only got red color. I do not like it.

女2： 你买衣服真麻烦。
Nǐ mǎi yīfu zhēn máfan.

You are such a trouble when shopping for dresses.

(二)

女1: 这两条裙子哪条好?
Zhè liǎng tiáo qúnzi nǎ tiáo hǎo?
Which of these two skirts is better?

女2: 我喜欢这条,颜色、样子都好看。
Wǒ xǐhuan zhè tiáo, yánsè、yàngzi dōu hǎokàn.
I like this one. Both the color and the pattern look nice.

女1: 我不喜欢这条,这条裙子太短了。
Wǒ bù xǐhuan zhè tiáo, zhè tiáo qúnzi tài duǎn le.
I do not like this one. It's too short.

女2: 现在穿短裙子的人很多。
Xiànzài chuān duǎn qúnzi de rén hěn duō.
Short skirts are popular nowadays.

女1: 我知道,可是我还是喜欢穿长一点儿的裙子。
Wǒ zhīdào, kěshì wǒ háishi xǐhuan chuān cháng yìdiǎnr de qúnzi.
I know, however, I still prefer longer skirts.

女2: 这条比那条长,你喜欢这条吗?
Zhè tiáo bǐ nà tiáo cháng, nǐ xǐhuan zhè tiáo ma?
This one is longer than that one. Do you like it?

女1: 也不喜欢,颜色不好看。
Yě bù xǐhuan, yánsè bù hǎokàn.
I do not like the color.

8 这件衣服很漂亮
This Dress Is Very Pretty

女2： 你喜欢什么颜色的衣服？
Nǐ xǐhuan shénme yánsè de yīfu?
What colors do you like?

女1： 我喜欢淡黄色的。
Wǒ xǐhuan dàn huángsè de.
I like light yellow.

(三) 买衣服 Shopping of clothes

王红喜欢买衣服，特别喜欢买便宜衣服。每个星期天她都去商场，看见便宜的衣服就买。她家里有很多衣服，可是合适的衣服不多。有的太大，有的太小，有的太长，有的太短。有的颜色不好看，有的样子不好看。现在王红明白了，买便宜的衣服没有好处。她打算卖掉一些旧衣服，然后去买合适的新衣服。

Wang Hong enjoys buying clothes, especially cheap clothes. She goes for shopping every Sunday and would buy cheap clothes whenever she sees them. She has a lot of clothes at home, however, not so many are suitable for her. Some are too large, some too small, some too long or too short. Some have problems with colors and some with designs. Now she understands that it does no good to buy cheap clothes. So she plans to sell some old dresses and buy new suitable ones.

注释 | Annotation

1. 是绿色的。It is green.

"色"表示"颜色",其他如"红色、黄色"。

"色" means "颜色" (color). Other examples: "红色" (red)、"黄色" (yellow).

2. 我应该穿中号的。My size is medium.

在表示衣服的尺寸时,中国人常用"号(儿)"来表示。衣服一般被分为小号(S)、中号(M)、大号(L)三种。更大的还可以叫"加肥加大号"(XL、XXL……)。

"号(儿)" is used to measure the size of clothes in China. Clothes are generally classified into small size(S)、medium size(M) and large size (L). Extra large size is called "加肥加大"(XL, XXL...).

语法 | Grammar

1. 这条比那条长

"A 比 B + 形容词"是最常用的一种表示比较的句式。如:

"A 比 B + adjective" is the most commonly used structure to express comparison. For example:

8 这件衣服很漂亮
This Dress Is Very Pretty

（1）这件比那件大。

This one is larger than that one.

（2）这本书比那本书贵。

This book is more expensive than that one.

（3）他比我努力。

He works harder than I do.

2. 有的……，有的……

几个"有的"连用，表示人或事物中的一部分。如：

"有的" can be used individually or jointly to express part of a group of people or some of the mentioned objects. For example:

（1）有的在看书，有的在做练习。

Some (people) are reading and some are doing exercises.

（2）有的大，有的小。

Some are big and some are small.

练习 | Exercises

1. 听录音，选择合适的回答：

Listen to the record and choose a proper answer:

（1）A. 不错，多少钱？

B. 我知道。

（2）A. 是吗？我试试。

B. 我喜欢这件，颜色、样子都好看。

(3) A. 没有大号的。
　　B. 对不起，只有小号的。
(4) A. 绿色对你很合适。
　　B. 你喜欢绿色。

2. 用"有的……有的……"把下列词组连成句子：
   Use "有的……有的……" to join the following phrases into complete sentences:
   (1) 这些衣服　　太长　　　　太短
   (2) 这些房间　　太大　　　　太小
   (3) 朋友们　　　喜欢喝红茶　喜欢喝绿茶
   (4) 客人们　　　吃饺子　　　吃面条
   (5) 同学们　　　听现代音乐　听古典音乐
   (6) 我们　　　　吃中餐　　　吃西餐

3. 在下列句子里填上合适的词：
   Fill in the blanks with appropriate words:
   (1) 这杯咖啡比那杯咖啡（　　　）。
   (2) 这本书比那本书（　　　）。
   (3) 这件衣服比那件衣服（　　　）。
   (4) 这条裙子比那条裙子（　　　）。
   (5) 听音乐比做作业（　　　）。
   (6) 饺子比面条（　　　）。

8 这件衣服很漂亮
This Dress Is Very Pretty

4. 翻译：

Translation:

(1) 红　　绿　　黄

(2) 大号　　中号　　小号

(3) 好玩儿　　好吃　　好看

(4) 长　　短　　大　　小　　新　　旧

5. 看短文，选词语：

Choose the proper word to fill in the passage:

新　短　小　旧　合适　颜色　好处　明白　看见　特别

我喜欢买衣服，(1)___喜欢买便宜衣服。每个星期天我都去商场，(2)___便宜的衣服就买。我家里有很多衣服，可是 (3)___ 的衣服不多。有的太大，有的太 (4)___，有的太长，有的太 (5)___。有的 (6)___ 不好看，有的样子不好看。现在我 (7)___ 了，买便宜的衣服没有 (8)___。我打算卖掉一些 (9)___ 衣服，然后去买合适的 (10)___ 衣服。

6. 用下列词语续写：

Complete the passage with the following words:

我喜欢买衣服，……

参考词语：颜色　样子　大　小　长　短　大/中/小号
　　　　　合适　特别　好看

生词 | New Words

1	件	jiàn	（量）	measure word	一件衣服 / a dress 我买了三件衣服。 I've bought three dresses. 这件衣服多少钱？ How much is this dress?
2	颜色	yánsè	（名）	color	红颜色 / red 有很多种颜色 / many colors 你喜欢什么颜色？ Which color do you like?
3	小	xiǎo	（形）	small	小商店 / small shop 小房间 / small room 这件衣服有点儿小。 This garment is a little small.
4	穿	chuān	（动）	to take on; to wear	穿衣服 / put on clothes 穿绿色的衣服 wear green clothes 你喜欢穿什么颜色的衣服？ Which color of clothes do you like?
5	中（号）	zhōng (hào)	（形）	medium(size)	中号的衣服 medium size of clothes 有没有中号的衣服？ Do you have the medium size? 中号的太小了，我要大号的。 The medium size is too small. I want the big size.
6	裙子	qúnzi	（名）	skirt	一条裙子 / a skirt 穿裙子 / wear skirts 我喜欢穿裙子。 I like wearing skirts.
7	样子	yàngzi	（名）	looking; design	衣服的样子 / the look of a dress 裙子的样子 / the look of a skirt 这件衣服的样子很漂亮。 This dress is good-looking.

8 这件衣服很漂亮
This Dress Is Very Pretty

8	好看	hǎokàn	(形)	nice-looking	样子很好看 / nice-looking 颜色很好看。 The color is good-looking. 这件衣服很好看。 This dress is nice-looking.
9	短	duǎn	(形)	short	她喜欢穿短一点儿的裙子。 She likes to wear short skirts. 这件衣服有点儿短。 This dress is a little short.
10	比	bǐ	(介)	compare	这件衣服比那件好。 This dress is better than that one. 这个公园比那个公园大。 This park is bigger than that one. 这条裙子比那条裙子长。 This skirt is longer than that one.
11	有的	yǒude	(代)	some	有的长,有的短 some are long; some are short 有的大,有的小 some are big; some are small 那儿有很多人,有的是学生,有的是老师。 There're many people: some are students, and some are teachers.
12	黄	huáng	(形)	yellow	黄颜色 / yellow color 黄裙子 / a yellow skirt 他喜欢穿黄颜色的衣服。 He likes to wear yellow clothes.
13	卖掉	màidiào	(动)	to sell	卖掉衣服 / sell the clothes 卖掉不需要的书 sell books of no use 我卖掉了不需要的东西。 I've sold things of no use.
14	旧	jiù	(形)	old	旧书 / secondhand book 旧衣服 / worn clothes 我卖掉了很多旧衣服。 I've sold many worn clothes.
15	新	xīn	(形)	new	新书 / new book 新衣服 / new clothes 我有很多新朋友。 I have many new friends.

听力录音文本及参考答案

1. （1）这件衣服怎么样？
（2）这两件衣服哪件好？
（3）有中号的吗？
（4）绿颜色的怎么样？
（1）A　（2）B　（3）B　（4）A

2. 略。

3. 略。

4. 略。

5. （1）特别　　（2）看见　　（3）合适　　（4）小　　（5）短
（6）颜色　　（7）明白　　（8）好处　　（9）旧　　（10）新

6. 略。

9 你最喜欢哪个季节?
Nǐ zuì xǐhuan nǎ ge jìjié?
Which Season Do You Like Best?

句型 | Sentence Patterns

81. 春天 到了。
Chūntiān dào le.
Spring is here.

82. 你最喜欢哪个季节?
Nǐ zuì xǐhuan nǎ ge jìjié?
Which season do you like best?

83. 天气渐渐暖和了。
Tiānqì jiànjiàn nuǎnhuo le.
The weather is getting warmer.

84. 各种花都开了。
Gè zhǒng huā dōu kāi le.
Various kinds of plants are in bloom.

85. 树变成了绿色。
Shù biànchéng le lǜsè.
The trees turn green.

86. 风是够大的。
Fēng shì gòu dà de.
The wind is really strong.

87. 阳光很温和。
Yángguāng hěn wēnhé.
The sunshine is mild.

88. 秋天是旅游的好季节。
Qiūtiān shì lǚyóu de hǎo jìjié.
Autumn is a good season for traveling.

89. 气温不高也不低。
Qìwēn bù gāo yě bù dī.
The temperature is neither high nor low.

90. 今天是十八度。
Jīntiān shì shíbā dù.
It is eighteen degrees today.

9 你最喜欢哪个季节？
Which Season Do You Like Best?

课文 | Text

(一)（两位朋友在聊天 Two friends are chatting）

男1： 一年有四个季节，你最喜欢哪个季节？
Yì nián yǒu sì gè jìjié, nǐ zuì xǐhuan nǎ gè jìjié?
Among the four seasons of a year, which one do you like best?

男2： 我最喜欢春天。
Wǒ zuì xǐhuan chūntiān.
I like spring the best.

男1： 为什么？
Wèi shénme?
Why?

男2： 因为春天天气渐渐暖和了，各种花都开了，很漂亮。
Yīnwèi chūntiān tiānqì jiànjiàn nuǎnhuo le, gè zhǒng huā dōu kāi le, hěn piàoliang.
Because the weather turns warmer gradually in spring and there are blooms of all kinds. It is very pretty.

男1： 春天 经常 刮 风，风还特别大，我不喜欢
Chūntiān jīngcháng guā fēng, fēng hái tèbié dà, wǒ bù xǐhuan
春天。
chūntiān.

It is often windy in spring and the wind is especially strong. I do not like spring.

男2： 风 是 够 大 的， 不过，刮 风的 时间 不 长。
Fēng shì gòu dà de, búguò, guā fēng de shíjiān bù cháng.

The wind is indeed strong; however, it usually does not last long.

男1： 我 喜欢 秋天。
Wǒ xǐhuan qiūtiān.

I like autumn.

男2： 秋天 不刮 风 吗？
Qiūtiān bù guā fēng ma?

Isn't it windy in autumn?

男1： 秋天 也 刮 风，可是秋天的 风 比 春天 少。
Qiūtiān yě guā fēng, kěshì qiūtiān de fēng bǐ chūntiān shǎo.

It is also windy, but not as frequent as in spring.

男2： 秋天 天气 渐渐 冷 了，也 没有 花 了。
Qiūtiān tiānqì jiànjiàn lěng le, yě méiyǒu huā le.

It turns cold gradually in autumn. There are no flowers left.

9 你最喜欢哪个季节?
Which Season Do You Like Best?

(二)

女： 今天气温多少度？
Jīntiān qìwēn duōshao dù?
What is the temperature today?

男： 十八度。
Shíbā dù.
18°C.

女： 昨天是二十二度，今天比昨天冷一点儿。
Zuótiān shì èrshí'èr dù, jīntiān bǐ zuótiān lěng yìdiǎnr.
It was 22°C yesterday, so today is a little colder than yesterday.

男： 是的，昨天晚上下雨了。
Shìde, zuótiān wǎnshang xià yǔ le.
Yes, it rained last night.

女： 雨下得大吗？
Yǔ xià de dà ma?
Did it rain heavily?

男： 够大的。
Gòu dà de.
It was heavy indeed.

女： 今年秋天的雨水真多。
Jīnnián qiūtiān de yǔshuǐ zhēn duō.
We have a lot of rainfall this autumn.

男：是够多的。今天外边比较冷，你多穿一点儿衣服。
　　Shì gòu duō de. Jīntiān wàibian bǐjiào lěng, nǐ duō chuān yìdiǎnr yīfu.

Yes indeed. It is fairly cold outside today. Put on more clothes.

女：好，谢谢！
　　Hǎo, xièxie!

All right. Thank you!

（三）春天到了 Spring is here

春天到了，天气渐渐暖和了。公园里，各种花都开了，红的、绿的、黄的……真好看。马路旁边的树也变成了绿色。太阳很好，阳光很温和，气温不高也不低，真是旅游的好季节。

孩子们非常高兴，他们穿着漂亮的衣服出去玩儿，有的在公园里看花，有的去参观博物馆，有的去动物园看动物，还有的去书店买有意思的书……他们喜欢春天，他们在春天里玩儿得高兴极了。

Spring is here. The weather is getting warmer gradually. There are all kinds of blooms in the park, red ones, green ones, yellow ones..., really nice looking. The trees on the roadside trun green too. The sun is shining and the sunshine is mild. The temperature is neither high nor low. It is really a good season for travelling.

9 你最喜欢哪个季节？
Which Season Do You Like Best?

The children are very happy. They are dressed nicely and go outdoors. Some go to enjoy flowers in the park, some go to visit the museum and some go to the zoo to see the animals, and the others go to bookstores for interesting books .... They like spring. They are very happy in spring.

注释 | Annotation

1. 一年有四个季节，你最喜欢哪个季节？Among the four seasons of a year, which one do you like best?

   一年的四个季节是：春天、夏天、秋天、冬天。

   Four seasons of a year are: spring, summer, autumn, winter.

2. 风是够大的。The wind is indeed strong.

   "是"表示确定的语气，在这里要重读。

   "是", showing the tone of confirm, should be accentuated here.

语法 | Grammar

1. 够大的

   "够……的" 中间加形容词,表示程度比较高。常用于口语。如:

   Adjectives are inserted in the structure "够……的" to express the degree or level is fairly high. It often appears in colloquial Chinese. For example:

   (1) 够冷的

   fairly cold

   (2) 够便宜的

   fairly cheap

   (3) 够舒服的

   fairly comfortable

2. 今天比昨天冷一点儿。

   "A 比 B + 形容词 + 一点儿",表示比较的双方有一点儿差别。如:

   "A 比 B + adjectives + 一点儿", a structure to express the slight difference between the A and B which are in comparison. For example:

   (1) 这件衣服比那件衣服贵一点儿。

   This suit is somewhat more expensive than that one.

9 你最喜欢哪个季节？
Which Season Do You Like Best?

（2）我的汉语比他的汉语好一点儿。

My Chinese is a bit better than his.

（3）这条裙子比那条裙子长一点儿。

This skirt is a bit longer that that one.

练习 | Exercises

1. 听后选择下句：

Listen to the record and choose a proper sentence to respond:

（1）A. 春天天气渐渐暖和了。
　　B. 秋天刮风的时间不长。
　　C. 我最喜欢春天。

（2）A. 昨天二十二度。
　　B. 今天是十八度。
　　C. 我发烧了，有三十八度。

（3）A. 是够多的。
　　B. 外面没有下雨。
　　C. 雨下得很大。

（4）A. 秋天是旅游的好季节。
　　B. 秋天天气渐渐冷了。
　　C. 秋天的阳光很温和。

2. 完成对话：

Complete the following dialogues:

(1) A：外面天气怎么样？

　　B：_____。

　　A：风大吗？

　　B：_____。

　　A：冷不冷？

　　B：_____。

(2) A：今天多少度？

　　B：_____。

　　A：够冷的。

　　B：_____。

　　A：我们不要去公园了。

　　B：_____。

(3) A：你喜欢哪个季节？

　　B：_____。

　　A：为什么？

　　B：_____。

　　A：我不喜欢。风太大。

　　B：_____。

(4) A：公园里的花开了吗？

　　B：_____。

　　A：好看吗？

　　B：_____。

9 你最喜欢哪个季节?
Which Season Do You Like Best?

A：树呢？

B：_____。

3. 选词填空：

Choose the right word to fill in the following blanks:

够热的　够长的　够大的　够漂亮的　够贵的　够舒服的

(1) 这条裙子（　　　）。

(2) 昨天晚上的雨（　　　）。

(3) 你的家真（　　　）。

(4) 这本书真（　　　）。

(5) 今天的天气（　　　）。

(6) 这间房间（　　　）。

4. 把括号中的词放入合适的位置：

Put the words in brackets in the proper positions:

(1) A 今天 B 比昨天 C 冷 D。（一点儿）

(2) 你 A 多 B 穿 C 衣服 D。（一点儿）

(3) 春天经常 A 刮风，风 B 特别大，C 我 D 不喜欢春天。（还）

(4) A 秋天天气渐渐 B 冷了，C 没有 D 花了。（也）

(5) 秋天阳光 A 很温和，B 气温不高 C 不低，D 是旅游的好季节。（也）

5. 回答问题：

Answer the following questions:

（1）一年有几个季节？

（2）你最喜欢哪个季节？为什么？

（3）今天气温多少度？

（4）外面冷不冷？下雨了吗？

（5）北京的春天是不是经常刮风？

（6）今天是比昨天冷一点儿吗？

6. 参考下列词语说一段话：

Make a speech with the following words:

题目：我最喜欢的季节

参考词语： 春天　夏天　秋天　冬天　开花

　　　　　 暖和　刮风　温和　雨水　冷　热

生词 | New Words

1	春天	chūntiān	（名）	spring	春天来了。/ The spring comes. 春天风很大。 Winds are strong in spring. 春天很少下雨。 It seldom rains in spring.
2	季节	jìjié	（名）	season	四个季节 / four seasons 一年有四个季节。 There are four seasons in a year. 你喜欢哪个季节？ Which season do you prefer?

9 你最喜欢哪个季节?
Which Season Do You Like Best?

3	渐渐	jiànjiàn	(副)	gradually	渐渐明白了 gradually understand 天气渐渐冷了。 It's getting cold.
4	暖和	nuǎnhuo	(形)	warm	暖和的春天 / warm spring 暖和的天气 / warm weather 天气渐渐暖和了。 It's getting warm.
5	开	kāi	(动)	to bloom	开花 / blossom 没开花 / not blossom 各种花都开了。 All the flowers blossomed.
6	树	shù	(名)	tree	一棵(kē, measure word)树 a tree 大树 / big tree 小树 / little tree 马路边有很多树。 There're lots of trees on both sides of the road.
7	变成	biànchéng	(动)	to turn	变成绿色 / turn green 变成朋友 / become friends 他变成了老师。 He becomes a teacher.
8	够	gòu	(副)	fairly; enough	够远的 / far enough 够热的 / hot enough 生词够多的 enough new words
9	阳光	yángguāng	(名)	sunshine	阳光充足(chōngzú, abundant) abundant sunshine 没有阳光 / no sunshine 今天的阳光很好。 Nice sunshine today.
10	温和	wēnhé	(形)	mild; moderate	温和的阳光 / mild sunshine 温和的天气 / mild weather 秋天的阳光很温和。 Sunshine in autumn is mild.

11	秋天	qiūtiān	(名)	autumn	秋天的风比春天的少。 There are fewer winds in autumn than spring 秋天天气渐渐冷了。 It's getting cold in autumn. 我最喜欢的季节是秋天。 Autumn is my favorite season.
12	旅游	lǚyóu	(名)	travel	经常旅游 / often travel 去北京旅游 / travel to Beijing 你打算去哪儿旅游？ Where are you going to travel?
13	气温	qìwēn	(名)	temperature	最高气温 the highest temperature 气温很低 / low temperature 今天的气温是多少？ What's the temperature today?
14	高	gāo	(形)	high	特别高 / extremely high 太高了 / too high 他的体温很高,应该去医院。 He has a high temperature. He should go to hospital.
15	低	dī	(形)	low	很低 / very low 有点儿低 / a little bit low 今天的气温低极了。 Temperature today is extremely low.
16	度	dù	(量)	*measure word*	十八度 / 18 degrees 今天是十八度。 It's 18 degrees today. 明天多少度？ What's the temperature tomorrow?
17	昨天	zuótiān	(名)	yesterday	昨天下雨了。 It rained yesterday. 昨天很冷。 It was very cold yesterday. 昨天你干什么了？ What did you do yesterday?

9 你最喜欢哪个季节?
Which Season Do You Like Best?

18	雨水	yǔshuǐ	(名)	rainwater; rainfall	雨水充足(chōngzú, abundant) abundant rainfall 春天的雨水不多。 Rainfall is not much in spring. 今年秋天的雨水真不少。 Rainfall is quite abundant this autumn.
19	外边	wàibian	(名)	outside	外边天气不错。 It's fine weather outside. 外边渐渐暖和了。 It's getting warm outside. 他们在外边干什么? What are they doing outside?
20	比较	bǐjiào	(副)	rather	比较低 / rather low 比较高兴 / quite happy 今天比较冷。 It's rather cold today.
21	太阳	tàiyáng	(名)	sun	温和的太阳 / mild sunshine 秋天太阳很温和。 Sunshine is very mild is autumn. 今天是晴天,太阳很好。 It's sunny and fine weather today.
22	孩子	háizi	(名)	child	孩子们 / the children 孩子们很高兴。 The children are very happy. 孩子喜欢在外边玩儿。 Children like playing outside.
23	书店	shūdiàn	(名)	bookstore	一家书店 / a bookstore 去书店 / go to the bookstore 书店有很多有意思的书。 Many interesting books can be found in the bookstore.

听力录音文本及参考答案

1. (1) 你最喜欢哪个季节?
   (2) 今天气温多少度?
   (3) 今年秋天的雨水真多。

(4) 你为什么不喜欢秋天？
(1) C　(2) B　(3) A　(4) B

2. 略。

3. (1) 够长的　(2) 够大的　　(3) 够漂亮的
   (4) 够贵的　(5) 够热的　　(6) 够舒服的

4. (1) D　(2) C　(3) B　(4) C　(5) C

5. 略。

6. 略。

10 Qù yīyuàn kànkan bìng ba!
去医院看看病吧!
Go to See a Doctor Then!

句型 | Sentence Patterns

91. 我 有点儿咳嗽。
Wǒ yǒudiǎnr késou.
I have got a slight cough.

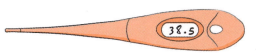

92. 量量 体温 吧!
Liángliang tǐwēn ba!
Let's take your temperature then!

93. 他发烧了,三十八度五。
Tā fā shāo le, sānshíbā dù wǔ.
He has a fever, 38.5 °C.

94. 不要紧,吃点儿药就好了。
Bú yàojǐn, chīdiǎnr yào jiù hǎo le.
It is not so serious. He would be fine after taking some medicine.

95. 他最近身体一直不好。
Tā zuìjìn shēntǐ yìzhí bù hǎo.
He has been in bad conditions recently.

96. 去医院看看病吧！
Qù yīyuàn kànkan bìng ba!
Go to see a doctor then!

97. 工作比较忙，太累了。
Gōngzuò bǐjiào máng, tài lèi le.
I am busy with the work and feel very tired.

98. 你要注意早点儿休息。
Nǐ yào zhùyì zǎo diǎnr xiūxi.
You should take a rest.

99. 怎么才能保持身体健康？
Zěnme cái néng bǎochí shēntǐ jiànkāng?
How can one keep good health?

100. 保持精神愉快，不要生气。
Bǎochí jīngshén yúkuài, búyào shēngqì.
Keep in good mood, and avoid anger.

10 去医院看看病吧！
Go to See a Doctor Then!

课文 | Text

(一) （在医院 In the hospital）

男1： 你哪儿不舒服？
Nǐ nǎr bù shūfu?
What's wrong with you?

男2： 我 感冒了，头很 疼。
Wǒ gǎnmào le, tóu hěn téng.
I have got a flu, and a serious headache.

男1： 咳嗽吗？
Késou ma?
Do you have a cough?

男2： 有一点儿。
Yǒu yìdiǎnr.
A little bit.

男1： 几天了？
Jǐ tiān le?
How long has it been like this?

男2： 两 天了。
Liǎng tiān le.
Two days already.

男1： 量过 体温吗？
Liángguo tǐwēn ma?
Have you taken your temperature?

135

男2： 量了，我不发烧，三十六度五。
Liáng le, wǒ bù fā shāo, sānshíliù dù wǔ.

Yes, I do not have a fever, 36.5 °C.

男1： 不要紧，吃点儿药就好了。
Bú yàojǐn, chīdiǎnr yào jiù hǎo le.

It does not matter much. You would be all right after taking some medicine.

男2： 中药还是西药？
Zhōngyào háishi xīyào?

Is it Chinese medicine or western medicine?

男1： 吃中药吧，中药比较温和。
Chī zhōngyào ba, zhōngyào bǐjiào wēnhé.

Take Chinese medicine then. Chinese medicine is mild.

男2： 好，谢谢！
Hǎo, xièxie!

All right. Thank you!

男1： 你还要多喝水，多吃水果。
Nǐ hái yào duō hē shuǐ, duō chī shuǐguǒ.

You should drink more water and eat more fruits.

男2： 我知道了。
Wǒ zhīdào le.

I see.

10 去医院看看病吧!
Go to See a Doctor Then!

(二)

男: 我最近身体一直不好。
Wǒ zuìjìn shēntǐ yìzhí bù hǎo.

I have been in bad conditions recently.

女: 怎么不好?
Zěnme bù hǎo?

What's wrong?

男: 不想吃饭,睡觉也不好。
Bù xiǎng chī fàn, shuì jiào yě bù hǎo.

I do not feel like eating and cannot sleep well, either.

女: 是不是工作太累了?
Shì bu shì gōngzuò tài lèi le?

Does the work make you tired?

男: 最近比较忙,每天晚上十二点才能睡觉。
Zuìjìn bǐjiào máng, měi tiān wǎnshang shí'èr diǎn cái néng shuì jiào.

I am busy recently, and cannot go to bed till 12 o'clock at night.

女: 你要注意早点儿休息。
Nǐ yào zhùyì zǎo diǎnr xiūxi.

You should go to bed earlier.

男: 我一定注意。
Wǒ yídìng zhùyì.

I would definitely try.

女： 再去医院看看病，吃点儿药。
Zài qù yīyuàn kànkan bìng, chī diǎnr yào.

Go to the hospital to see a doctor and take some medicine.

男： 我 不喜欢吃药，注意休息 就 行 了。
Wǒ bù xǐhuan chī yào, zhùyì xiūxi jiù xíng le.

I do not like taking medicine. I will be fine with more rest.

（三）保持身体健康 To keep in good health

怎么才能保持身体健康？我的办法是：第一，天气冷了，多穿衣服，天气热了，少穿衣服；第二，多喝水，多吃水果，少喝酒，少吃药；第三，工作不能太累，注意休息；第四，经常出去玩儿，或者去公园，或者参观博物馆，或者和朋友一起吃饭，或者……；第五，保持精神愉快，不要生气。

我的朋友对我说，还应该经常锻炼身体。可是我不锻炼身体，身体也非常好。

How can we keep in good health? I offer my own methods here. Firstly, put on more clothes when it turns cold and less clothes when it is hot. Secondly, more water and fruits, less alcohol and medicine. Thirdly, do not work too much to get tired; paying attention to having a good rest. Fourthly, going outdoors to the park, the museum, or dining with friends, and etc. Fifthly, keep in pleasant mood and avoid anger.

10 去医院看看病吧!
Go to See a Doctor Then!

My friends tell me that I shall do more exercises to build up my body, but I am strong even without physical excercises.

注释 | Annotation

1. 不要紧，吃点儿药就好了。 It does not matter much. You would be all right after taking some medicine.

"不要紧"的意思是情况不严重，不用担心。

"不要紧" means "the situation is not serious, don't worry".

2. 早点儿休息　go to bed earlier

"早、晚、快、慢"都可以和"点儿"一起用，后面再加上动词，表示动作发生得"早、晚、快、慢"。如：

"早""晚""快" and "慢" (early, late, quick, slow) can be used together with "点儿" (a bit). Verbs are added after it to express the status of actions which is "early, late, quick, slow". For example:

(1) 早点儿走

go earlier

(2) 晚点儿去

go later

3. 我的办法是：第一，……。I offer my own methods here, firstly...

"第"用来表示序数，加在数词前面。如：

"第" is used to indicate ordinal, added before numerals. For example:

(1) 第一

the first

(2) 第二十

the twentieth

(3) 第二十八

the twenty-eighth

(4) 第一百

the one hundredth

语法 | Grammar

1. 一直

主要有两个意思：一个意思表示顺着某个方面不变，另一个意思表示从过去某一时间到现在不变。如：

It has two meanings. One indicates direction and the other indicates time, the complete duration from the past to the present. For example:

10 去医院看看病吧！
Go to See a Doctor Then!

（1）一直往东走

　　all the way /straight towards the east

（2）他一直学习汉语。

　　He has been learning Chinese.

（3）他晚上一直听音乐。

　　He has been listening to music all the night.

2. 或者

"或者"是表示选择的连词，用在陈述句里。可以单独使用，也可以几个连用。如：

"或者" is a conjunction to indicate choices in a statement. It can be used either independently or jointly. For example:

（1）单用：你去或者我去都可以。

　　Independently: It is all right whether you or I go.

（2）连用：或者红的，或者绿的，我都喜欢。

　　Jointly: I like it whether it is red or green.

练习 | Exercises

1. 听录音，选择合适的回答：

Listen to the record and choose a proper answer:

（1）A. 量了，不发烧。

　　B. 我最近身体一直不好。

（2）A. 三十八度三。
　　B. 我一直休息。
（3）A. 不要紧，吃点儿药就好了。
　　B. 吃中药吧，中药比较温和。
（4）A. 工作比较忙，太累了。
　　B. 好，我会注意。
（5）A. 保持精神愉快，不要生气。
　　B. 这样才能保持健康。

2. 词语搭配：

Match the words in the two groups:

（1）量　　　　　看病
（2）锻练　　　　健康
（3）去医院　　　休息
（4）注意　　　　体温
（5）保持　　　　身体

3. 连词成句：

Connect the following words into complete sentences:

（1）他　　不好　　身体　　一直

_____

（2）附近　　住在　　一直　　他　　学校

_____

（3）往东走　　去　　一直　　动物园　　应该

_____

10 去医院看看病吧!
Go to See a Doctor Then!

(4) 上午　在　一直　图书馆　他　看书

_____

4. 完成对话:

Complete the following dialogues:

(1) A：你的脸很红，发烧了吧?

B：_____。

A：是感冒吗?

B：_____。

A：去医院看看病吧?

B：_____。

(2) A：我头有点儿疼，感冒了。

B：_____?

A：我不发烧。

B：_____。

A：多喝水，注意休息，再吃点儿药。

B：_____。

5. 替换练习:

Substitution exercises:

(1) 你<u>早点儿起床</u>。

　　晚　睡觉

　　快　吃

　　慢　喝

（2）他应该<u>慢点儿</u>说。

　　　　早　　去医院
　　　　快　　去打电话
　　　　晚　　告诉他

（3）<u>或者</u>去公园，<u>或者</u>参观博物馆。

　　　　去买东西　　去动物园
　　　　喝茶　　　　喝咖啡
　　　　买红色的　　买绿色的

6. 用下列格式介绍你保持健康的办法：

Introduce the ways you keep fit with the following structures:

参考句式：第一……，第二……，第三……
　　　　　或者……，或者……
　　　　　保持……，不要……

生词 | New Words

1	咳嗽	késou	（动）	to cough	我有点儿咳嗽。 I've got a slight cough. 我每天都咳嗽。 I cough every day.
2	量	liáng	（动）	to measure	量体温 / take one's temperature 你需要量一下体温。 You need to take your temperature.

10 去医院看看病吧!
Go to See a Doctor Then!

3	体温	tǐwēn	(名)	body temperature	你体温不高。/ You have no fever. 你现在的体温是多少? What's your body temperature now?
4	发烧	fā shāo		to have a fever	有点儿发烧 / have a light fever 我发烧了。/ I have a fever. 我不发烧,三十六度五。 I do not have a fever. 36.5℃.
5	要紧	yàojǐn	(形)	serious	不要紧 / not seriours 要紧吗?/ Is it serious? 不要紧,休息一下儿吧。 It's not serious. Have some rest.
6	药	yào	(名)	medicine	吃药 / take medicine 买药 / buy medicine 我不喜欢药。 I don't like taking medicine.
7	中药	zhōngyào	(名)	Chinese medicine	中药店 Chinese medicine pharmacy 吃中药 / take Chinese medicine 我应该吃点儿中药。 I should take some Chinese medicine.
8	西药	xīyào	(名)	Western medicine	吃西药 take Western medicine 你喜欢中药还是西药? Do you prefer Chinese medicine or Western medicine?
9	最近	zuìjìn	(副)	recently	最近很忙。/ Very busy recently. 最近去过哪儿? Where have you been recently? 最近我每天都在家里看书。 I've been reading at home these days.
10	忙	máng	(形)	busy	很忙 / very busy 不太忙 / not very busy 你最近忙吗? Are you busy recently?

145

11	累	lèi	（形）	tired	很累 / very tired 不累 / not tired 我很累。/ I'm very tired.
12	注意	zhùyì	（动）	to pay attention	注意休息 / take good rest 注意身体 pay attention to your health 你感冒了，要注意多喝水。 Since you've caught a cold, you should drink more water.
13	保持	bǎochí	（动）	to maintain	保持健康 / keep healthy 保持精神愉快 keep in good mood 请继续(jìxù, continue)保持。 Please keep up.
14	第一	dìyī	（数）	first	第一，……第二，……第三…… first...; second...; third... 保持健康要注意的是：第一，多喝水；第二，多吃水果；第三，多休息。 How can we keep in good health? Firstly, drink more water. Secondly, eat more fruits. Thirdly, take more rest.
15	精神	jīngshén	（名）	spirit	精神很好 / be in high spirits 今天我精神不错。 I'm in nice mood today.
16	愉快	yúkuài	（形）	pleasant; happy	精神愉快 / be in high spirits 每天很愉快 / happy every day 我过了一个愉快的星期天。 I had a pleasant Sunday.
17	生气	shēng qì		to be angry	很生气 / very angry 不要生气。/ Don't be angry. 你为什么生气？ Why are you angry?
18	水	shuǐ	（名）	water	喝水 / drink water 没有水了 / no more water 感冒的时候应该多喝水。 Drink more water when you've caught a cold.

10 去医院看看病吧！
Go to See a Doctor Then!

19	办法	bànfǎ	(名)	ways; means	好办法 / good idea 没有办法 / can't handle it 我有很多好办法。 I've lots of good ideas.
20	或者	huòzhě	(连)	or	我经常出去，或者去公园，或者去博物馆。 I often go outdoors to the park, or to the museum. 或者你来我家，或者我去你家，都可以。 I go to your house, or you come to my place. Both are OK. 我每天晚上都在家，或者看书，或者看电视。 I'm at home every night, reading books or watching TV.
21	锻炼	duànliàn	(动)	to exercise; to build up	锻炼身体 exercise one's body 你每天去哪里锻炼? Where do you do exercises every day? 我每天都去公园锻炼身体。 I go to the park to do exercises every day.

听力录音文本及参考答案

1. （1）量体温了吗？
   （2）发烧吗？
   （3）中药还是西药？
   （4）你要注意早点儿休息。
   （5）怎么才能保持身体健康？
   （1）A　（2）A　（3）B　（4）B　（5）A
2. （1）量体温
   （2）锻炼身体
   （3）去医院看病

(4) 注意休息

(5) 保持健康

3. (1) 他身体一直不好。

(2) 他一直住在学校附近。

(3) 去动物园应该一直往东走。

(4) 上午他一直在图书馆看书/他上午一直在图书馆看书。

4. 略。

5. 略。

6. 略。

11 鱼的味道怎么样?
Yú de wèidào zěnmeyàng?
How Is the Taste of the Fish?

句型 | Sentence Patterns

101. 您吃点儿什么? 这是菜单。
Nín chīdiǎnr shénme? Zhè shì càidān.

What would you like to eat? This is the menu.

102. 这里什么菜最有名?
Zhèli shénme cài zuì yǒumíng?

What is the most famous here?

103. 味道怎么样?
Wèidào zěnmeyàng?

How is the taste?

104. 辣子鸡丁和麻辣豆腐都不错。
Làzi jīdīng hé málà dòufu dōu búcuò.

Both chicken with chilli and spicy bean curd are good.

105. 我最喜欢吃鱼和素菜。
Wǒ zuì xǐhuan chī yú hé sùcài.

I like fish and vegetarian dish the best.

106. 我 不 能 吃辣 的。
Wǒ bù néng chī là de.

I do not eat spicy food.

107. 请 给我一碗 米饭。
Qǐng gěi wǒ yì wǎn mǐfàn.

Please give me a bowl of rice.

108. 这 碗 鸡蛋汤 有点儿 咸。
Zhè wǎn jīdàntāng yǒudiǎnr xián.

The egg soup is slightly salty.

109. 请 等一会儿，马上 就好。
Qǐng děng yíhuìr, mǎshàng jiù hǎo.

Please wait for a while. It would be ready soon.

110. 客人比较多，没有 座位了。
Kèrén bǐjiào duō, méiyǒu zuòwèi le.

There are many customers. No more seats available.

11 鱼的味道怎么样?
How Is the Taste of the Fish?

课文 | Text

(一)（在饭店点菜 Ordering food in the restaurant）

女: 您吃点儿什么？这是菜单。
Nín chīdiǎnr shénme? Zhè shì càidān.
What would you like to eat? This is the menu.

男: 这里什么菜最有名？
Zhèlǐ shénme cài zuì yǒumíng?
What is the most famous dish here?

女: 辣子鸡丁和麻辣豆腐都不错。
Làzi jīdīng hé málà dòufu dōu búcuò.
Both chicken with chilli and spicy bean curd are good.

男: 我喜欢吃豆腐，可是不能吃辣的。
Wǒ xǐhuan chī dòufu, kěshì bù néng chī là de.
I like bean curd, but not spicy.

女: 那您吃糖醋鱼吧，也很好。
Nà nín chī tángcùyú ba, yě hěn hǎo.
Then you can try sweet sour fish, also very good.

男: 好，我喜欢吃鱼。
Hǎo, wǒ xǐhuan chī yú.
All right. I like fish.

女: 还要别的吗？
Hái yào biéde ma?
Anything else?

男: 还要一个素菜。
Hái yào yí gè sùcài.

And a vegetarian dish.

女: 喝什么？
Hē shénme?

What would you like to drink?

男: 一杯橙汁。
Yì bēi chéngzhī.

A glass of orange juice.

女: 要汤吗？
Yào tāng ma?

Any soup?

男: 一碗鸡蛋汤，再要一碗米饭。
Yì wǎn jīdàntāng, zài yào yì wǎn mǐfàn.

Egg soup and a bowl of rice.

女: 请等一会儿，马上就好。
Qǐng děng yíhuìr, mǎshàng jiù hǎo.

Please wait for a while. They would be ready soon.

男: 谢谢！
Xièxie!

Thank you!

11 鱼的味道怎么样?
How Is the Taste of the Fish?

(二)

女: 鱼的味道 怎么样?
Yú de wèidào zěnmeyàng?
How is the taste of the fish?

男: 又 甜 又 酸, 味道 很 好。
Yòu tián yòu suān, wèidào hěn hǎo.
It is sweet and sour, tasty.

女: 汤 的味道好 不好?
Tāng de wèidào hǎo bu hǎo?
Is the taste of the soup good?

男: 汤 有点儿 咸 了。
Tāng yǒudiǎnr xián le.
The soup is slightly salty.

女: 真 对不起, 请 原谅。
Zhēn duìbuqǐ, qǐng yuánliàng.
I am really sorry for that.

男: 没 什么。
Méi shénme.
It is all right.

女: 欢迎 您 下次再来。
Huānyíng nín xià cì zài lái.
Hope to see you again.

（三）四川饭店 Sichuan Hotel

我喜欢吃辣的，经常去四川饭店吃饭。四川饭店的菜都辣极了，特别是辣子鸡丁和麻辣豆腐，是两个有名的辣菜，又辣又香，味道好极了。还有那儿的鱼，也是辣的，味道也不错。

四川饭店的客人比较多，经常没有座位，需要等一会儿。那儿的菜也比别的饭店贵。可是，我还是喜欢去那儿。我喜欢一边喝酒，一边吃菜，一边听音乐，真是舒服极了。

I like spicy food and often dine in Sichuan Hotel. The dishes in Sichuan Hotel are extremely spicy, particularly chicken with chilli and spicy bean curd. These are the two well-known dishes. They are spicy and tasty. The fish is spicy too, also delicious.

Sichuan Hotel is so popular with customers that seats are often not available. You need to wait before getting a seat there. The food there is also more expensive than other restaurants, but I still like to go there to dine. I enjoy drinking and eating while listening to music. It is really comfortable.

11 鱼的味道怎么样？
How Is the Taste of the Fish?

注释 | Annotation

1. 这里什么菜最有名？What is the most famous dish here?

"这里"和"这儿"的意思基本相同。同样，"那儿"也可以说成"那里"。

"这里" and "这儿" have the same meaning. Similarly, "那儿" can also be said as "那里".

2. 我喜欢吃豆腐，可是不能吃辣的。I like bean curd, but not spicy.

"辣的"在这里是指"辣的菜"，其他如"酸的""甜的""咸的"。

"辣的" means spicy dish here, other examples are "酸的" (sour), "甜的" (sweet), "咸的" (salty).

语法 | Grammar

1. 马上就好。

"马上"和"就"经常在一起用，强调情况就要发生。如：

"马上" and "就" are often used together to emphasize something is going to take place soon. For example:

（1）马上就要下雨了。

　　It is going to rain immediately.

（2）我马上就来。

　　I am coming immediately.

2. 有点儿咸了。

"有点儿+形容词"表示程度轻（如"有点儿累、有点儿忙"），"有点儿+形容词+了"表示不满意，形容词前还可以加上"太"，表示不满的程度较深。如：

"有点儿 + adjective" expresses a moderate degree or level ("有点儿累"[slightly tired], "有点儿忙"[slightly busy])."有点儿 + adjective + 了" suggests dissatisfaction. "太" can be added before the adjectives, showing great dissatisfaction. For example:

（1）有点儿甜了

　　slightly sweet

（2）有点儿太贵了

　　a bit too expensive

（3）有点儿太客气了

　　a bit over polite/courteous

11 鱼的味道怎么样？
How Is the Taste of the Fish?

练习 | Exercises

---

1. 听录音，选择合适的回答：

Listen to the record and choose a proper answer:

（1）A. 麻辣豆腐最有名。
　　 B. 您吃糖醋鱼吧。
　　 C. 我要一个素菜。

（2）A. 还要一碗鸡蛋汤。
　　 B. 我最喜欢吃鱼了。
　　 C. 真对不起，请原谅。

（3）A. 很好，又酸又甜。
　　 B. 有点儿太贵了。
　　 C. 豆腐有点儿咸了。

（4）A. 我最喜欢喝橙汁。
　　 B. 这碗汤有点儿辣。
　　 C. 我最喜欢吃辣子鸡丁。

（5）A. 真对不起，请原谅。
　　 B. 请等一会儿，马上就好。
　　 C. 欢迎您下次再来。

2. 选词填空：

Choose the right word to fill in the following blanks:

这　那　这儿（这里）　那儿（那里）　哪　哪儿

(1) 你去过四川饭店吗？（　　）的菜味道怎么样？
(2) 我们在（　　）吃吧，（　　）的菜不错。
(3) 这位是王老师，（　　）位是李老师。
(4) 你喜欢上海吗？（　　）的天气怎么样？
(5) 给你，（　　）是你的钥匙。
(6) 你是在（　　）出生的？
(7) 你的朋友是（　　）国人？

3. 用"有点儿……了"把下列词造成句子：

Use "有点儿……了" to join the following words into complete sentences:

(1) 这件衣服　　　贵
(2) 那碗汤　　　咸
(3) 豆腐　　　辣
(4) 糖醋鱼　　　甜
(5) 这个菜　　　酸
(6) 那条裙子　　　短

4. 完成对话：

Complete the following dialogues:

(1) A：您要点什么？
　　B：_____。

11 鱼的味道怎么样?
How Is the Taste of the Fish?

A：喝点什么？
B：＿＿＿＿＿＿＿＿＿＿＿＿＿＿＿。
A：还要别的吗？
B：＿＿＿＿＿＿＿＿＿＿＿＿＿＿＿。

(2) A：＿＿＿＿＿＿＿＿＿＿＿＿＿＿＿？
B：我咳嗽了，不能吃辣的。
A：＿＿＿＿＿＿＿＿＿＿＿＿＿＿＿。
B：好，我最喜欢吃豆腐。
A：＿＿＿＿＿＿＿＿＿＿＿＿＿＿＿。
B：谢谢，我也不能喝酒。

5. **参考下列词语说一段话：**

Make a speech with the following words:

题目：我喜欢的中国菜

参考词语：鱼　素菜　豆腐　有名　味道　辣　酸　甜
　　　　　咸　又……又……

生词 | New Words

| 1 | 菜单 | càidān | （名） | menu | 这是菜单。/ Here's the menu.
请您看一下菜单。
Please take a look at the menu.
有英文菜单吗？
Do you have a menu in English version? |

2	这里	zhèli	(代)	here	这里什么好吃？ What tasty food have you got here? 我在这里住了三年。 I've lived here for 3 years. 这里风景漂亮极了。 The landscapes are wonderful here.
3	有名	yǒumíng	(形)	famous	有名的饭店 a famous restaurant 有名的钢琴曲 a well-known piano tune 这里什么菜最有名？ What is the most famous dish here?
4	味道	wèidào	(名)	taste	味道很浓 / strong taste 味道怎么样？ How's the taste? 你喜欢什么味道的菜？ What kind of food do you like?
5	鱼	yú	(名)	fish	一条(tiáo, measure word)鱼 a fish 鱼的味道怎么样？ How's the taste of the fish? 我最喜欢吃鱼了。 I love eating fish.
6	素菜	sùcài	(名)	vegetarian dish	一个素菜 / a vegetarian dish 他只吃素菜。 He's a complete vegetarian. 很多孩子不喜欢吃素菜。 Many children dislike vegetarian dishes.
7	辣	là	(形)	hot	辣极了 / extremely hot 我不能吃辣的。 I can't eat spicy food. 这里的鱼也很辣。 The fish here is spicy too.

11 鱼的味道怎么样?
How Is the Taste of the Fish?

8	碗	wǎn	(名)	bowl	一个碗 / a bowl 碗里有水 / bowl with water 这个碗太小了。 This bowl is too small.
9	米饭	mǐfàn	(名)	rice	一碗米饭 / a boul of rice 您要米饭吗? Would you like rice? 他喜欢吃米饭。 He likes rice.
10	鸡蛋	jīdàn	(名)	egg	一个鸡蛋 / an egg 每天早上吃一个鸡蛋。 An egg each morning. 吃太多鸡蛋对健康不好。 Eating too many eggs is not good to health.
11	汤	tāng	(名)	soup	鸡蛋汤 / egg soup 鱼汤 / fish soup 他喝了一碗汤。 He had a bowl of soup.
12	咸	xián	(形)	salty	咸菜 Chinese pickled vegetables 咸鸡蛋 / salted egg 鱼汤太咸了。 The fish soup is too salty.
13	马上	mǎshàng	(副)	immediately	他马上来。 He'll come immediately. 我马上要去上海了。 I'm going to Shanghai soon. 请等一会儿,马上就好。 Wait a moment. It'll be OK soon.
14	座位	zuòwèi	(名)	seat	一个座位 / a seat 没有座位 / no seat 饭店的座位不多。 Seats are not enough in the restaurant.

15	菜	cài	(名)	dish	有名的菜 / famous dish 我喜欢吃辣的菜。 I like spicy food. 你要什么味道的菜？ What kind of food do you like?
16	豆腐	dòufu	(名)	bean curd	一块(kuài, measure word)豆腐 / a piece of bean crud 豆腐汤 / bean curd soup 用(yòng, use)豆腐可以做很多菜。 Many dishes are made of bean curd.
17	橙汁	chéngzhī	(名)	orange juice	一杯橙汁 a cup of orange juice 一瓶橙汁 a bottle of orange juice 喝橙汁对身体有好处。 Orange juice is good to health.
18	酸	suān	(形)	sour	太酸了 / too sour 橙汁有点儿酸。 The orange juice is slightly sour. 糖醋鱼又酸又甜。 The sweet sour fish is sweet and sour.
19	辣子鸡丁	làzi jīdīng		chicken with chilli	
20	麻辣豆腐	málà dòufu		spicy bean curd	
21	糖醋鱼	tángcùyú		sweet sour fish	

专有名词：

Proper noun:

四川	Sìchuān	Sichuan Province

11 鱼的味道怎么样？
How Is the Taste of the Fish?

听力录音文本及参考答案

1. （1）您吃点儿什么？
   （2）还要别的吗？
   （3）鱼的味道怎么样？
   （4）你最喜欢吃什么菜？
   （5）我点的菜请快一点儿。
   （1）C　（2）A　（3）A　（4）C　（5）B

2. （1）那儿/那里
   （2）那儿/那里，那儿/那里 或者 这儿/这里，这儿/这里
   （3）那
   （4）那儿/那里
   （5）这
   （6）哪儿
   （7）哪

3. 略。
4. 略。
5. 略。

12 你可以试试喝减肥茶
Nǐ kěyǐ shìshi hē jiǎnféichá
You Can Try the Diet Tea

句型 | Sentence Patterns

---

111. 我最近越来越胖。
Wǒ zuìjìn yuèláiyuè pàng.
I have grown in weight recently.

112. 太 胖了对身体 没有好处。
Tài pàng le duì shēntǐ méiyǒu hǎochù.
Overweight does no good to the health.

113. 有 什么 办法可以减 肥吗?
Yǒu shénme bànfǎ kěyǐ jiǎn féi ma?
Is there any way to keep fit?

114. 我 天天 跑步。
Wǒ tiāntiān pǎobù.
I jog every day.

115. 我 还是这么 胖。
Wǒ háishi zhème pàng.
I am still too big.

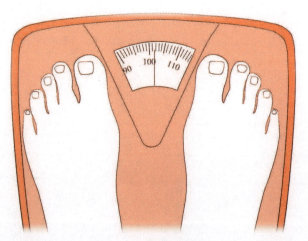

12 你可以试试喝减肥茶
You Can Try the Diet Tea

116. 你应该少吃甜的东西。
Nǐ yīnggāi shǎo chī tián de dōngxi.
You should take less sweet food.

117. 你可以试试喝减肥茶。
Nǐ kěyǐ shìshi hē jiǎnféichá.
You can try the diet tea.

118. 我决定减肥。
Wǒ juédìng jiǎn féi.
I decide to keep fit.

119. 我正在做减肥体操呢!
Wǒ zhèngzài zuò jiǎn féi tǐcāo ne!
I am doing the weight reducing exercise!

120. 一点儿作用也没有。
Yìdiǎnr zuòyòng yě méiyǒu.
It has no effect at all.

课文 | Text

(一)

女: 你最近有点儿胖了。
Nǐ zuìjìn yǒudiǎnr pàng le.
You have grown a little bit recently.

男: 是,我越来越胖。
Shì, wǒ yuèláiyuè pàng.
Yes, I am gaining weight.

女: 太胖了对身体没有好处。
Tài pàng le duì shēntǐ méiyǒu hǎochù.
Overweight does no good to the health.

男: 有什么办法可以减肥吗?
Yǒu shénme bànfǎ kěyǐ jiǎnféi ma?
Is there any way to reduce my weight?

女: 你应该每天锻炼身体。
Nǐ yīnggāi měi tiān duànliàn shēntǐ.
You should do physical exercises every day.

男: 我天天跑步,还是这么胖。
Wǒ tiāntiān pǎobù, háishi zhème pàng.
I jog every day, however, I remain heavy.

女: 你喜欢吃甜的东西吧?
Nǐ xǐhuan chī tián de dōngxi ba?
Do you like sweet food?

12 你可以试试喝减肥茶
You Can Try the Diet Tea

男: 我喜欢吃糖。
Wǒ xǐhuan chī táng.
I like sweet candies.

女: 你要少吃糖。
Nǐ yào shǎo chī táng.
You should take in less sweets.

男: 是不是还要少吃饭?
Shì bu shì hái yào shǎo chī fàn?
Also less rice?

女: 少吃饭对身体也不好。
Shǎo chī fàn duì shēntǐ yě bù hǎo.
Less rice is not beneficial to the health, either.

男: 还有别的办法减肥吗?
Hái yǒu bié de bànfǎ jiǎn féi ma?
Is there any other ways to reduce my weight?

女: 你可以试试喝减肥茶。
Nǐ kěyǐ shìshi hē jiǎnféichá.
You can try diet tea.

男: 好,我试试。
Hǎo, wǒ shìshi.
All right. I would try.

(二)

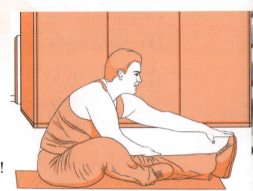

女：你在干什么？
Nǐ zài gàn shénme?

What are you doing?

男：我正在做减肥体操呢！
Wǒ zhèngzài zuò jiǎn féi tǐcāo ne!

I am doing exercise to reduce weight!

女：你打算减肥吗？
Nǐ dǎsuàn jiǎn féi ma?

Do you plan to reduce weight?

男：是，我最近越来越胖。
Shì, wǒ zuìjìn yuèláiyuè pàng.

Yes, I have gained weight recently.

女：做体操有用吗？
Zuò tǐcāo yǒuyòng ma?

Will the exercise work?

男：一点儿作用也没有，我还是这么胖。
Yìdiǎnr zuòyòng yě méiyǒu, wǒ háishi zhème pàng.

No effect at all. I remain the same in weight.

女：胖也很好看，不一定要减肥。
Pàng yě hěn hǎokàn, bù yídìng yào jiǎn féi.

It can be also good-looking to be fleshy. No necessity to reduce the weight.

12 你可以试试喝减肥茶
You Can Try the Diet Tea

（三）减肥 Weight reduction

我最近越来越胖，我决定减肥。同学们告诉我很多减肥的办法：第一，锻炼身体，做减肥体操；第二，少吃饭，少吃甜的东西；第三，喝减肥茶；第四，吃减肥药。

各种办法我都试过了。我天天跑步，天天做体操。我每天只吃两顿饭，也不吃糖。我买了减肥茶，也买了减肥药，每天喝，每天吃，可是一点儿作用也没有，我没有瘦，还是这么胖。

I have gained weight recently. I decide to control my weight. My classmates give me a lot of advices. Firstly, do physical exercises to reduce the weight. Secondly, take less rice and sweet food. Thirdly, drink diet tea. Fourthly, take some medicine of weight control.

I have tried all the ways. I jog every day and do exercises daily. I even have only two meals a day and do not take sweets. I drink diet tea and take medicine daily. However, there is no effect at all. My figure remains the same as before.

注释 | Annotation

1. 我还是这么胖。I remain heavy.

指示代词"这么"表示程度高。如：

The demonstrative pronoun "这么" indicates the degree or level is high. For example:

（1）天气这么好。

The weather is so good.

（2）汤这么咸。

The soup is so salty.

2. 我没有瘦。I have not got thin.

副词"没有"可以用在形容词前，肯定式是"瘦了"。

"没有" can be used before adjectives. The affirmative form is "瘦了"。

语法 | Grammar

1. 越来越胖

"越来越……"用在形容词语前，表示程度随着时间的推移而提高，后可加"了"。如：

12 你可以试试喝减肥茶
You Can Try the Diet Tea

"越来越……" expresses the degree or level increases as time goes on. "了" can be added after it. For example:

(1) 越来越瘦

    getting slimmer

(2) 越来越好

    getting better

(3) 越来越冷了

    getting colder

(4) 越来越不爱吃糖了

    taking less and less sweets

2. 天天跑步

"天天"是"天"的重叠式，意思是"每天"。其他如"年年""人人"：

"天天" is the reduplicated form of "天", meaning every day. Other examples are "年年""人人"：

(1) 天天吃药

    take medicine every day

(2) 年年去中国

    go to China every year

(3) 人人都喜欢漂亮。

    Everybody likes to be pretty.

3. 正在……呢

表示动作正在持续。也说"在……呢"。如：

This form is used to indicate that the action is in the process and in a continuing state. It can also be said as "在……呢". For example:

(1) 他正在喝水呢。

He is drinking.

(2) 我正在打电话呢。

I am making a call.

(3) 小王在做体操呢。

Xiao Wang is doing exercise.

4. 可是

连词，表示转折。如：

A conjunction to express transition. For example:

(1) 我很喜欢这件衣服，可是没有大号的。

I like this clothes very much, however, there are no large size.

(2) 今天天气很好，可是我没有时间出去玩儿。

The weather today is nice, however, I have no time to go to play outside.

12 你可以试试喝减肥茶
You Can Try the Diet Tea

练习 | Exercises

1. 听录音，选择合适的回答：

Listen to the record and choose a proper answer:

（1）A. 是，我最近越来越胖。
　　　B. 是，我喜欢做体操。

（2）A. 每天锻炼身体。
　　　B. 我打算减肥。

（3）A. 我喜欢吃糖。
　　　B. 我少吃甜的东西。

（4）A. 越多越好。
　　　B. 少吃饭对身体不好。

（5）A. 好，我可以。
　　　B. 好，我试试。

（6）A. 不有用。
　　　B. 一点儿作用也没有。

（7）A. 胖也很好看，不一定要减肥。
　　　B. 各种办法都试过了。

2. 用"越来越……"完成下列句子：

Use "越来越……" to complete the following sentences:

（1）最近工作（　　）了。

（2）商店里的东西（　　）了。

(3) 春天到了，天气（　　）了。
(4) 风（　　）了。
(5) 他学习（　　）。
(6) 最近他身体一直不好，（　　）。

3. 选择合适的词组连成句子：

Choose the right phrases and connect them into complete sentences:

    A   B
(1) 医院里的人 那么好
(2) 这本书   这么辣
(3) 今天的天气 那么多
(4) 买火车票   这么没意思
(5) 这碗汤   那么麻烦

4. 翻译并造句：

Translate and make sentences:
(1) 不胖也不瘦
(2) 不冷也不热
(3) 不高也不低
(4) 不大也不小
(5) 不长也不短
(6) 不咸也不淡

12 你可以试试喝减肥茶
You Can Try the Diet Tea

5. 选词填空：

Choose the right words to fill in the blanks:

瘦　少　甜　药　喝　顿　试　锻炼　办法　决定
可是　还是　天天

我最近越来越胖，我 (1) 减肥。同学们告诉我很多减肥的 (2) ：第一，(3) 身体，做减肥体操；第二，(4) 吃饭，少吃 (5) 的东西；第三，(6) 减肥茶；第四，吃减肥 (7) 。

各种办法我都 (8) 过了。我 (9) 跑步，我每天只吃两 (10) 饭，也不吃糖。我还喝减肥茶，吃减肥药，(11) 一点儿作用也没有，我没有 (12) ，(13) 这么胖。

6. 参考下列格式说一段话:

Make a speech with the following structures:

题目：减肥的好办法

参考格式：第一……，第二……，第三……，第四……
　　　　　少……　天天……

生词 | New Words

| 1 | 越来越 | yuèláiyuè | (to get)more and more... | 越来越好
better and better
越来越贵
more and more expensive
我的身体越来越好。
I'm getting healthier. |

2	胖	pàng	（形）	overweight; fleshy; fat	很胖 / very fat 不太胖 / not too fat 我越来越胖。 I'm getting more and more weight.
3	减肥	jiǎn féi		to reduce weight	减肥药 weight-reducing medicine 减肥茶 / diet tea 我要减肥。 I want to lose weight.
4	跑步	pǎo bù		to jog	我喜欢跑步。 I like running. 他每天跑步。 He does running every day.
5	这么	zhème	（代）	such; so	这么贵 / so expensive 这么好 / so good 喝了很多减肥茶，我还是这么胖。 Though I've taken lots of diet tea, I'm still so fat.
6	少	shǎo	（形）	little	少看电视 / watch less TV 你的衣服太多，你应该少买新衣服。 You have so many clothes that you should buy less new clothes. 少吃饭对身体不好。 Less meal is bad to health.
7	决定	juédìng	（动）	to decide	决定了吗？ Have you decided? 我决定学一年英语。 I decided to learn English for a year. 我决定10月去北京。 I've decided to go to Beijing in October.

12 你可以试试喝减肥茶
You Can Try the Diet Tea

8	体操	tǐcāo	(名)	physical exercise	做体操 do gymnastic exercises 减肥体操 weight-reducing gymnastic exercises 做体操对身体很好。 Gymnastic exercises are very good to our health.
9	作用	zuòyòng	(名)	effect; function	有作用。/ It works. 没有作用。 It doesn't work. 做体操一点儿作用也没有。 Gymnastic exercises don't work at all.
10	顿	dùn	(量)	*measure word*	吃一顿饭 / have a meal 一天三顿饭 three meals a day 我每天只吃两顿饭。 I only take two meals a day.
11	没有	méiyǒu	(副)	not	没有买 / didn't buy 没有来 / didn't come 做减肥体操没有作用。 Gymnastic exercises don't work.
12	瘦	shòu	(形)	thin; slim	很瘦 / very thin 太瘦了 / too thin 她越来越瘦。 She becomes thinner and thinner.
13	可是	kěshì	(连)	but	我每天喝减肥茶,可是越来越胖。 Though I take diet tea every day, I'm still getting fatter and fatter. 这件衣服很漂亮,可是她不喜欢。 This dress is so beautiful, but she doesn't like it.

听力录音文本及参考答案

1. （1）你打算减肥吗？
   （2）有什么办法可以减肥吗？
   （3）你喜欢吃甜的东西吧？
   （4）是不是还要少吃饭？
   （5）你可以试试喝减肥茶。
   （6）做体操有用吗？
   （7）我越来越胖了，我要减肥。
   （1）A （2）A （3）A （4）B （5）B （6）B （7）A

2. 略。

3. （1）医院里的人那么多。
   （2）这本书这么没意思。
   （3）今天的天气那么好。
   （4）买火车票那么麻烦。
   （5）这碗汤这么辣。

4. 略。

5. （1）决定　　（2）办法　　（3）锻炼　　（4）少
   （5）甜　　　（6）喝　　　（7）药　　　（8）试
   （9）天天　　（10）顿　　　（11）可是　　（12）瘦
   （13）还是

6. 略。

13. 他是一个体育爱好者
Tā shì yí gè tǐyù àihàozhě
He Is a Sport Enthusiast

句型 | Sentence Patterns

121. 他正在操场上打网球呢！
Tā zhèngzài cāochǎng shang dǎ wǎngqiú ne!
He is playing tennis on the playground!

122. 打网球是他最喜欢的体育活动。
Dǎ wǎngqiú shì tā zuì xǐhuan de tǐyù huódòng.
Tennis is his favorite sport.

123. 他是一个体育爱好者。
Tā shì yí gè tǐyù àihàozhě.
He is a sport enthusiast.

124. 跑步、游泳、滑冰，他样样都行。
Pǎo bù、yóu yǒng、huá bīng, tā yàngyàng dōu xíng.

He is good at everything: jogging, swimming and skating.

125. 他从来不得病。
Tā cónglái bù dé bìng.

He is never sick.

126. 我从来没打过棒球。
Wǒ cónglái méi dǎguo bàngqiú.

I have never played baseball before.

127. 他一年四季都锻炼身体。
Tā yì nián sì jì dōu duànliàn shēntǐ.

He keeps on physical exercises throughout the year.

128. 我要去打太极拳了。
Wǒ yào qù dǎ tàijíquán le.

I am going to practice Taiji.

129. 无论刮风天还是下雨天，他都不停止。
Wúlùn guā fēng tiān háishì xià yǔ tiān, tā dōu bù tíngzhǐ.

He never stops (exercising) whether it is windy or rainy.

130. 他五十多岁了，身体比年轻人还好。
Tā wǔshí duō suì le, shēntǐ bǐ niánqīngrén hái hǎo.

He is over fifty years old, but is even in better health than young people.

13 他是一个体育爱好者
He Is a Sport Enthusiast

课文 | Text

(一) （两个朋友在谈话 Two friends are chatting）

女：小 王 在 哪儿？
Xiǎo Wáng zài nǎr?
Where is Xiao Wang?

男：他 正在 操场 上
Tā zhèngzài cāochǎng shang
打 网球 呢！
dǎ wǎngqiú ne!
He is playing tennis on the playground.

女：他那么喜欢打 网球？
Tā nàme xǐhuan dǎ wǎngqiú?
Does he like tennis so much?

男：他喜欢 活动，天天下午 都 打一会儿网球。
Tā xǐhuan huódòng, tiāntiān xiàwǔ dōu dǎ yíhuìr wǎngqiú.
He is active, and plays tennis for a while every afternoon.

女：除了打 网球，他还 喜欢别的体育活动 吗？
Chúle dǎ wǎngqiú, tā hái xǐhuan bié de tǐyù huódòng ma?
Besides tennis, what other sports does he like?

男：跑步、游泳、滑冰，他 样样 都 行。
Pǎo bù、 yóu yǒng、 huá bīng, tā yàngyàng dōu xíng.
He is good at everything: jogging, swimming and skating.

女： 他一年四季都锻炼身体。
Tā yì nián sì jì dōu duànliàn shēntǐ.
He keeps on physical exercises throughout the year.

男： 他是一个体育爱好者。
Tā shì yí gè tǐyù àihàozhě.
He is a sports enthusiast.

女： 他的身体一定很健康。
Tā de shēntǐ yídìng hěn jiànkāng.
He must be very healthy then.

男： 是，他从来不得病。
Shì, tā cōnglái bù dé bìng.
Yes, he is never sick.

(二)

男1： 你经常锻炼身体吗？
Nǐ jīngcháng duànliàn shēntǐ ma?
Do you often do physical exercises?

男2： 是，我经常做体育活动。
Shì, wǒ jīngcháng zuò tǐyù huódòng.
Yes, I often go for sports.

男1： 你最喜欢的活动是什么？
Nǐ zuì xǐhuan de huódòng shì shénme?
What is your favorite sport?

13 他是一个体育爱好者
He Is a Sport Enthusiast

男2： 打棒球。
Dǎ bàngqiú.
Baseball.

男1： 我从来没打过棒球，有意思吗？
Wǒ cónglái méi dǎguo bàngqiú, yǒu yìsi ma?
I have never played baseball. Is it interesting?

男2： 有意思极了，你跟我一起去看看吧！
Yǒu yìsi jí le, nǐ gēn wǒ yìqǐ qù kànkan ba!
Very interesting. You can come along with me to have a look!

男1： 现在不行，我还有事。
Xiànzài bù xíng, wǒ hái yǒu shì.
Not now. I have something else to do.

男2： 也去锻炼身体吗？
Yě qù duànliàn shēntǐ ma?
Some physical exercises?

男1： 是，我要去打太极拳。
Shì, wǒ yào qù dǎ tàijíquán.
Yes, I am going to practice Taiji.

男2：你这么年轻也喜欢打太极拳吗？
Nǐ zhème niánqīng yě xǐhuan dǎ tàijíquán ma?
Why do you like practicing Taiji which is not supposed to be an activity for young men?

男1：我已经四十多岁了，不年轻了。
Wǒ yǐjīng sìshí duō suì le, bù niánqīng le.
I am already over forty, not that young any more.

（三）体育活动 Sports

王老师非常喜欢体育活动，他是一个体育爱好者。打网球、打棒球、跑步、滑冰、游泳……他样样都行。每天早上你可以看见他在校园里跑步，每天下午你又可以看见他在操场上打球。一年四季，无论刮风天还是下雨天，他都不停止。因为王老师天天锻炼，保持了身体健康。他很少感冒，很少去医院，从来没得过大病，也从来不吃药。他已经五十多岁了，身体比年轻人还好。

Mr. Wang(teacher) likes sports very much. He is a sport enthusiast. He is good at almost all sports: tennis, baseball, jogging, skating, swimming... You can see him jogging in the school yard every morning. You can see him play ball games on the playground every afternoon. Whether it is windy or rainy, he never stops throughout the year. Mr. Wang keeps his good health because he

13 他是一个体育爱好者
He Is a Sport Enthusiast

keeps on physical exercises every day. He seldom catches a flu, and seldom goes to hospital. He is never seriously ill or takes medicine. He is in his fifties, but is even in better health than young men.

注释 | Annotation

1. 他样样都行。He is good at everything.

   "样"是量词，重叠形式"样样"是"每一样"的意思。后面常用"都"。如：

   "样" is a measure word. The reduplicated form "样样" means "每一样". It if often followed by "都". For example:

   (1) 样样都会

      to know everything

   (2) 样样都吃

      to eat everything

2. 他一年四季都锻炼身体。He keeps on physical exercises throughout the year.

   "一年四季"即一年四个季节。

   "一年四季" means the four seasons of a year.

3. 我从来没打过棒球。I have never played beseball.

"没"是副词"没有"的省略。

"没" is an adverb, the simplified form of "没有"。

4. 四十多岁　over forty years old

数词"多"加在数目之后,表示概数。

The numeral "多" is added after numbers to indicate an approximate number.

语法 | Grammar

1. 从来

"从来"用在否定句中,否定动作、行为的发生。"从来"后可以用"不",也可以用"没(有)"。用"没"的时候,动词后一般要有"过"。如:

"从来" is used in negative sentences to negate an action or behavior. "从来" can be followed by "不" or "没(有)." When "没" is used, "过" must also be used. For example:

a. 从来+不+动词+宾语

从来+不+verb+object

从来不吃药

to take medicine never

13 他是一个体育爱好者
He Is a Sport Enthusiast

b. 从来＋没有＋动词＋过＋宾语

从来＋没有＋verb＋过＋object

从来没有吃过药

to have never taken medicine

2. 无论……还是……，都……

这个格式表示在任何条件、情况下，结果都不会变。"无论"和"还是"的后面可以是名词，也可以是动词。如：

This structure indicates that the result would not change under any conditions or circumstances. "无论" and "还是" can have both nouns and verbs after it. For example:

（1）无论你还是我，都不知道这件事。

　　　Neither you nor I know about this matter.

（2）无论去还是不去，都行。

　　　It is all right whether to go or not to go.

练习 | Exercises

1. 听录音，选择意思正确的句子：

Listen to the record and choose the sentence that match the record：

（1）A. 他最喜欢体育活动。

　　　B. 他很喜欢打网球。

（2）A. 他会很多体育运动。
　　　B. 他滑冰滑得不太好。
（3）A. 他每天都锻炼身体。
　　　B. 下大雨的时候，他不去锻炼身体。
（4）A. 他是个年轻人。
　　　B. 他身体很健康。

2. 替换练习：

Substitution exercises:

（1）<u>他</u>从来不<u>听音乐</u>。

　　小王　　锻炼身体
　　王红　　吃辣的
　　我　　　喝咖啡
　　她　　　做减肥体操

（2）<u>我</u>从来没<u>去过医院</u>。

　　我　　　打网球
　　老五　　吃西餐
　　小王　　学英语
　　他　　　喝酒

3. 翻译：

Translation:

（1）滑冰、游泳，他样样都喜欢。
（2）无论英语还是法语，他都不会。
（3）无论喜欢还是不喜欢，你都应该锻炼身体。

13 他是一个体育爱好者
He Is a Sport Enthusiast

（4）无论刮风还是下雨，他天天都跑步。

（5）他一年四季都锻炼身体。

（6）他一年四季工作都很忙。

4. 用否定式回答问题：

Use the negative form to answer the following questions:

（1）你去医院了吗？

（2）你洗衣服了吗？

（3）学校放假了吗？

（4）他参观博物馆了吗？

5. 完成对话：

Complete the following dialogues:

（1）A：你喜欢体育活动吗？

　　　B：_____。

　　　A：你喜欢什么活动？

　　　B：_____。

（2）A：_____？

　　　B：他在操场上打网球呢。

　　　A：_____？

　　　B：他网球打得不错。

　　　A：_____？

　　　B：除了打网球，他也喜欢跑步和游泳。

　　　A：_____？

　　　B：对，他一年四季都锻炼身体。

6. 参考下列词语说一段话：

Make a speech with the following words:

题目：我最喜欢的体育活动

参考词语：打　网球　跑步　游泳　滑冰　棒球　太极拳
　　　　　锻炼　健康　无论……还是……，都……

生词 | New Words

1	操场	cāochǎng	（名）	playground	在操场上 / on the playground 他在操场上呢。 He's on the playground. 操场上有很多孩子。 Many children are on the playground.
2	打	dǎ	（动）	to play	打网球 / play tennis 打篮球(lánqiú, basketball) play basketball 你会打棒球吗？ Can you play baseball?
3	网球	wǎngqiú	（名）	tennis	打网球 / play tennis 我没打过网球。 I've never played tennis.
4	体育	tǐyù	（名）	sports	体育课 / PE class 体育场(chǎng, field) / stadium 他喜欢体育。 / He likes sports.
5	活动	huódòng	（名）	activity	体育活动 / sports activity 你最喜欢的活动是什么？ What's your favorite activity? 今天下午学校有什么活动？ What the school's activity this afternoon?

13 他是一个体育爱好者
He Is a Sport Enthusiast

6	爱好者	àihàozhě	(名)	enthusiast	体育爱好者 / sports enthusiast 音乐爱好者 / music enthusiast 我是一个流行音乐爱好者。 I'm a pop music enthusiast.
7	游泳	yóu yǒng		to swim	我每个星期六都去游泳。 I go swimming every Saturday. 经常游泳对身体有好处。 Swimming often is good to our health. 我游了两个小时泳了。 I have been swimming for 2 hours.
8	滑冰	huá bīng		to skate	你会滑冰吗？/ Can you skate? 滑了一次冰 / skate once 他滑冰滑得很好。 He skates very well.
9	样	yàng	(量)	measure word	样样都会 capable of everything 样样都吃 eat every kind of food 他样样都行。 He's good at everything.
10	从来	cónglái	(副)	always	从来不吃药 never take medicine 我从来没有去过法国。 I've never been to France. 他从来没有打过网球。 He's never played tennis.
11	得	dé	(动)	to get	得病 / get sick 得了感冒 / caught cold 他从来不得病。 He never gets sick.
12	棒球	bàngqiú	(名)	baseball	打棒球 / play baseball 棒球爱好者 baseball hobbyist 你看过棒球比赛(bǐsài, competition)吗？ Have you seen a baseball competition?

13	太极拳	tàijíquán	（名）	Taiji	打太极拳 / play Taiji 学太极拳 / learn Taiji 他太极拳打得很好。 He plays Taiji very well.
14	无论	wúlùn	（连）	no matter what	无论春天还是秋天，他每天早上都打太极拳。 Whether it is spring or autumn, he plays Taiji every morning. 无论大卫还是王红，都喜欢听音乐会。 Both David and Wang Hong love listening to music.
15	停止	tíngzhǐ	（动）	to stop	停止跑步 / stop running 停止锻炼 / stop exercising 这件事不能停止。 This matter cannot stop.
16	年轻	niánqīng	（形）	young	年轻人 / young people 年轻的老师 / young teacher 他比我年轻。 He is younger than me.
17	多	duō	（数）	more	十多年 / over ten years 二十多个人 over twenty people 我们老板已经五十多岁了。 Our boss is over fifty.

听力录音文本及参考答案

1. （1）打网球是他最喜欢的体育活动。
   （2）跑步、游泳、滑冰，他样样都行。
   （3）无论刮风天还是下雨天，他都不停止锻炼身体。
   （4）他天天锻炼，保持了身体健康，身体比年轻人还好。
   （1）B （2）A （3）A （4）B

2. 略。　　3. 略。　　4. 略。
5. 略。　　6. 略。

14 希望以后继续合作
Xīwàng yǐhòu jìxù hézuò
Wish We Would Further Our Cooperation in the Future

句型 | Sentence Patterns

131. 昨天 晚上 我休息得很 好。
Zuótiān wǎnshang wǒ xiūxi de hěn hǎo.

I had a very good rest last night.

132. 讨论 两家 公司的 合作问题。
Tǎolùn liǎng jiā gōngsī de hézuò wèntí.

To discuss about the cooperation between the two companies.

133. 请 介绍一下贵公司的 产品。
Qǐng jièshào yíxià guì gōngsī de chǎnpǐn.

Please introduce the products of your company.

134. 能 看看 说明书 吗?
Néng kànkan shuōmíngshū ma?

Can I have a look at the product manual?

135. 质量已经达到了国际先进水平。
Zhìliàng yǐjīng dádào le guójì xiānjìn shuǐpíng.

The quality has already reached the advanced international standards.

136. 先看样品，然后再讨论。
Xiān kàn yàngpǐn, ránhòu zài tǎolùn.

(I want to) first look at the sample before discussing.

137. 我不能马上决定。
Wǒ bù néng mǎshàng juédìng.

I cannot decide immediately.

138. 价格很合适。
Jiàgé hěn héshì.

The prices are reasonable.

139. 出口水果、啤酒。
Chūkǒu shuǐguǒ、píjiǔ.

To export fruits and beer.

140. 进口电视和冰箱。
Jìnkǒu diànshì hé bīngxiāng.

To import television and refrigerator.

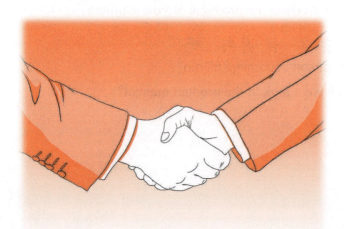

14 希望以后继续合作
Wish We Would Further Our Cooperation in the Future

课文 | Text

(一)

男1: 您好，马丁 先生！
Nín hǎo, Mǎdīng xiānsheng!
Hello, Mr. Martin!

男2: 你好，王 先生！
Nǐ hǎo, Wáng xiānsheng!
Hello, Mr. Wang!

男1: 昨天 晚上 休息得好吗？
Zuótiān wǎnshang xiūxi de hǎo ma?
Did you have a good rest last night?

男2: 休息得很好，谢谢！
Xiūxi de hěn hǎo, xièxie!
Yes, thank you!

男1: 餐厅 的 饭菜 怎么样？
Cāntīng de fàncài zěnmeyàng?
How is the food in the restaurant?

男2: 也很 好，中餐、西餐都有，我 很 满意。
Yě hěn hǎo, zhōngcān、xīcān dōu yǒu, wǒ hěn mǎnyì.
Good. They have both Chinese and western food. I am very satisfied.

男 1: 我们 今天 上午 讨论 两家 公司的合作问题，
Wǒmen jīntiān shàngwǔ tǎolùn liǎng jiā gōngsī de hézuò wèntí,

可以吗？
kěyǐ ma?

Is it all right for us to discuss about the cooperation between our companies this morning?

男 2: 可以，在哪儿讨论？
Kěyǐ, zài nǎr tǎolùn?

Sure. Where shall we hold the discussion?

男 1: 在二楼。
Zài èr lóu.

On the second floor.

男 2: 几点钟开始？
Jǐ diǎn zhōng kāishǐ?

When shall we start?

男 1: 九点半。
Jiǔ diǎn bàn.

At half past nine.

(二)

男: 请 介绍 一下贵公司的 产品。
Qǐng jièshào yíxià guì gōngsī de chǎnpǐn.

Please introduce the products of your company.

女: 我们 生产 冰箱。
Wǒmen shēngchǎn bīngxiāng.

We produce refrigerators.

14 希望以后继续合作
Wish We Would Further Our Cooperation in the Future

男： 能 看看 产品 说明书 吗？
Néng kànkan chǎnpǐn shuōmíngshū ma?
Can I take a look at the product manual?

女： 可以，请看。
Kěyǐ, qǐng kàn.
Sure, here it is.

男： 产品 质量怎么样？
Chǎnpǐn zhìliàng zěnmeyàng?
How about the quality of the products?

女： 产品 质量很好，已经达到了国际先进 水平。
Chǎnpǐn zhìliàng hěn hǎo, yǐjīng dádào le guójì xiānjìn shuǐpíng.
The quality of the products is very good. It has reached the advanced international standards.

男： 我们 很需要冰箱， 不过我不能 马上 决定。
Wǒmen hěn xūyào bīngxiāng, búguò wǒ bù néng mǎshàng juédìng.
We are in bad need of refrigerators, however, I cannot decide immediately.

女： 您是不是需要看看 样品？
Nín shì bu shì xūyào kànkan yàngpǐn?
Do you need to see the sample?

男: 是，我需要看样品。
Shì, wǒ xūyào kàn yàngpǐn.
Yes, I need to see the sample.

女: 希望您能满意。
Xīwàng nín néng mǎnyì.
Hope you would be satisfied.

男: 我先看样品，然后我们再讨论。
Wǒ xiān kàn yàngpǐn, ránhòu wǒmen zài tǎolùn.
I would like to see the sample first, then we can discuss about it.

女: 好，请跟我走。
Hǎo, qǐng gēn wǒ zǒu.
All right. Please follow me.

(三) 合作 Cooperation

二〇一五年三月十六日上午九点半，日本A公司的平田先生和中国B公司的王先生讨论了两家公司的合作问题。

A公司希望出口冰箱和电视，进口水果和啤酒。B公司希望出口水果和啤酒，进口日本生产的冰箱和电视。两个公司以前也合作过，产品的质量都很好，价格也很合适，他们一直合作得很愉快。他们希望以后继续合作。

Mr. Hirata from the Japanese company A and Mr. Wang from

14 希望以后继续合作
Wish We Would Further Our Cooperation in the Future

the Chinese company B discuss about the cooperation between their companies at 9：30 a.m. on Mar.16th, 2015. Company A intend to export refrigerators and televisions and import fruits and beer. Company B intend to export fruits and beer and import Japan-made refrigerators and televisions. Two companies have cooperated before. The quality of the products is very good, and the prices are reasonable, too. They have always been in pleasant cooperation. They hope further their cooperation in the future.

注释 | Annotation

1. 两家公司　two companies

　　"家"在这里是量词。

　　"家" is a measure word here.

2. 请介绍一下贵公司的产品。Please introduce the products of your company.

　　"贵"除了用于问人的姓名外（贵姓），也用在"国家、公司、学校"等名词前，表示尊敬。如：

　　"贵", besides the usage of inquiring for names of other people (贵姓), can be used before nouns like "国家" (country), "公司" (company) to indicate respect. For example:

　　（1）贵国

　　　　your (respected) country

(2) 贵公司

your (respected) company

(3) 贵校

your (respected) school

语法 | Grammar

1. 介绍一下

动词后加"一下"表示一种轻松的语气,或表示动作经历的时间短。如:

"一下" is added after verbs to suggest a light tone, or to indicate a short duration of the action. For example:

(1) 讨论一下

to have some discussion

(2) 看一下

to take a look

(3) 等一下

to wait a moment

2. 我先看样品,然后我们再讨论。

"先……然后……再……"是一个常用句式,表示动作的先后顺序。如:

14 希望以后继续合作

Wish We Would Further Our Cooperation in the Future

"先……然后……再……" is a frequent sentence pattern to express the order of actions. For example:

(1) 我们先去上海,然后再去广州。

　　We go to Shanghai first, and then Guangzhou.

(2) 他先去银行,然后我们再去商店。

　　He goes to the bank, and then we go to the store.

练习 | Exercises

1. 听录音,选择合适的回答:

Listen to the record and choose a proper answer:

(1) A. 休息得很好,谢谢!

　　B. 我不想休息。

(2) A. 中餐和西餐。

　　B. 我很满意。

(3) A. 九点半。

　　B. 在二楼。

(4) A. 可以,请看。

　　B. 说明书不错。

(5) A. 已经达到了国际先进水平。

　　B. 我想看看样品。

(6) A. 希望您能满意。

　　B. 我先看样品,然后再讨论。

2. 完成对话：

Complete the following dialogues:

（1）A：贵公司生产什么产品？

　　B：_____。

　　A：质量怎么样？

　　B：_____。

　　A：能先看看样品吗？

　　B：_____。

（2）A：这是你们的产品吗？

　　B：_____。

　　A：我想看一下说明书。

　　B：_____。

　　A：我很希望跟你们合作。

　　B：_____。

3. 选择合适的词连成词组：

Choose the right words to join into phrases:

　　　　A　　　　　　　B
（1）介绍　　　　　合作问题
（2）讨论　　　　　冰箱
（3）看看　　　　　大米
（4）进口　　　　　说明书
（5）出口　　　　　产品
（6）生产　　　　　电视

14 希望以后继续合作

Wish We Would Further Our Cooperation in the Future

4. 把下列句子按顺序排列：

Arrange the following sentences in right order:

A. 他的公司生产电视机和冰箱。

B. 平田先生来到中国，和A公司讨论两家的合作问题。

C. 平田先生在日本一家公司工作。

D. 公司要出口这些产品。

E. 他们的产品质量很好，已达到了国际先进水平。

5. 选词填空：

Choose the word to fill up:

以前　出口　进口　合适　继续　合作　质量　愉快

昨天上午，日本A公司的平田先生和中国B公司的王先生讨论了两家公司的 (1) 问题。

A公司希望 (2) 冰箱和电视，进口水果和啤酒。B公司希望出口水果和啤酒，(3) 日本生产的冰箱和电视。两个公司 (4) 也合作过，产品的 (5) 都很好，价格也很 (6)，他们一直合作得很 (7)。他们希望以后 (8) 合作。

6. 翻译：

Translation:

(1) 我以前来过中国。

(2) 以前我住在上海，现在住在北京。

(3) 两家公司以前经常合作。

(4) 我以前喜欢吃辣的，最近经常咳嗽，不吃了。

(5) 我知道你以前天天锻炼身体。

7. 参考下列词语说一段话：

Make a speech with the following words:

题目：A公司和B公司的合作

参考词语：出口　进口　讨论　合作　产品　说明书　质量

生词 | New Words

1	讨论	tǎolùn	（动）	to discuss	讨论问题 / discuss questions 先讨论，然后决定。 First discuss, and then decide. 我们今天讨论什么？ What do we discuss today?
2	合作	hézuò	（动）	to cooperate	公司的合作 cooperation between companies 两国的合作 cooperation between two countries 我们今天讨论两个公司的合作问题。 We discuss the cooperation between the two companies today.
3	问题	wèntí	（名）	question	有问题吗？ Is there any question? 有什么问题？ What's the problem? 我们先讨论第一个问题。 We will discuss the first problem.

14 希望以后继续合作
Wish We Would Further Our Cooperation in the Future

4	介绍	jièshào	（动）	to introduce	介绍一下 make an introduction 请介绍一下你的公司。 Please introduce your company. 我给你介绍我的朋友。 I will introduce my friends to you.
5	一下	yíxià	（数量）	while	等一下 wait a while 看一下 / look a while 请读一下课文。 Please read the book for a while.
6	产品	chǎnpǐn	（名）	product	公司的产品 products of the company 我们的产品质量很好。 Our products have good quality. 请介绍一下你们的产品。 Please introduce your products.
7	说明书	shuōmíng shū	（名）	instruction manual	有说明书吗？ Do you have the introduction manual? 请看说明书。 Please read the introduction manual. 能看看产品说明书吗？ Can I look at the introduction manual?
8	质量	zhìliàng	（名）	quality	质量很好 / good quality 质量不好 / bad quality 我们的产品质量很好。 Our products have good quality.

9	达到	dádào	(动)	to reach	达到很高的水平 reach high level 达到先进水平 reach advanced level 我们的产品质量很好,已经达到了国际先进水平。 The quality of the products is very good. It has reached the international standard.
10	先进	xiānjìn	(形)	advanced	先进水平 / advanced level 先进技术(jìshù, technology) / advanced technology 我们的产品质量已经达到了国际先进水平。 The quality of the products is very good. It has reached the international standard.
11	水平	shuǐpíng	(名)	level	水平很高 / high level 达到很高水平 reach high level 达到世界先进水平 reach advanced world levels
12	样品	yàngpǐn	(名)	sample	看样品 / look at the sample 这是我们样品。 This is our sample. 我需要看看样品。 I need to see the sample.
13	价格	jiàgé	(名)	price	价格很高 / high price 价格合适 / reasonable price 他们公司的产品质量很好,价格也比较合适。 The products of their company have good quality and reasonable price.

14 希望以后继续合作
Wish We Would Further Our Cooperation in the Future

14	出口	chūkǒu	(动)	to export	出口冰箱 exported refrigerators 出口电视 / exported TVs A公司希望出口冰箱和电视，B公司希望出口水果和啤酒。 Company A intends to export refrigerators and televisions while company B intends to export fruits and beer.
15	进口	jìnkǒu	(动)	to import	进口电视 / imported TVs 进口冰箱 imported refrigerators
16	生产	shēngchǎn	(动)	to produce	日本生产的电视质量不错。 The televisions produced by Japan have good quality. 你们公司生产什么产品？ What does your company produce? 我们的产品是A公司生产的。 Our products are produced by company A.
17	以前	yǐqián	(名)	before; previously	以前我不认识他。 I didn't know him before. 以前你学过汉语吗？ Did you study Chinese before? 以前我没去过动物园。 I haven't been to the zoo before.
18	希望	xīwàng	(动)	to hope	希望你高兴。 Hope you can be happy. 我很希望你来中国。 I hope you can visit China. 希望我们以后继续合作。 I hope we can cooperate in the future.

207

专有名词:

Proper noun:

| 平田 | Píngtián | Hirata |

听力录音文本及参考答案

1. （1）昨天晚上休息得好吗？
   （2）餐厅的饭菜怎么样？
   （3）我们今天在哪儿讨论？
   （4）能看看产品说明书吗？
   （5）产品质量怎么样？
   （6）您是不是需要看看样品？
   （1）A （2）B （3）B （4）A （5）A （6）B

2. 略。

3. （1）介绍产品   （2）讨论合作问题
   （3）看看说明书   （4）进口大米/冰箱
   （5）出口冰箱/大米   （6）生产电视/冰箱

4. C A D E B

5. （1）合作   （2）出口   （3）进口   （4）以前
   （5）质量   （6）合适   （7）愉快   （8）继续

6. 略。

7. 略。

15 Wǒ de Zhōngwén jìnbù hěn kuài
我的中文进步很快
My Chinese Standard Improves Rapidly

句型 | Sentence Patterns

141. 您是什么时候来中国的？
Nín shì shénme shíhou lái Zhōngguó de?
When did you come to China?

142. 我在北京大学学习汉语。
Wǒ zài Běijīng Dàxué xuéxí Hànyǔ.
I am studying Chinese at Peking University.

143. 现在你的汉语水平怎么样？
Xiànzài nǐ de Hànyǔ shuǐpíng zěnmeyàng?
How is your Chinese at present?

144. 还看不懂中文报纸。
Hái kàn bu dǒng Zhōngwén bàozhǐ.
I can not read Chinese newspaper yet.

145. 你能 看懂《人民日报》了，太好了！
Nǐ néng kàndǒng 《Rénmín Rìbào》 le, tài hǎo le!

You can read the *People's Daily*. It is great!

146. 了解国际新闻和国内大事。
Liǎojiě guójì xīnwén hé guónèi dàshì.

To understand international news and domestic affairs.

147. 看 到 商品 信息。
Kàn dào shāngpǐn xìnxi.

To notice commodity information.

148. 你学习真努力！
Nǐ xuéxí zhēn nǔlì!

You are really hardworking!

149. 因为 天天 看报纸，所以 中文 进步 很 快。
Yīnwèi tiāntiān kàn bàozhǐ, suǒyǐ Zhōngwén jìnbù hěn kuài.

Thanks to the daily newspaper reading, my Chinese improves very fast.

150. 我还能 看电视 呢！
Wǒ hái néng kàn diànshì ne!

I can understand the TV programs as well!

15 我的中文进步很快
My Chinese Standard Improves Rapidly

课文 | Text

(一)

男1： 你是什么时候来中国的?
Nǐ shì shénme shíhou lái Zhōngguó de?
When did you come to China?

男2： 我是去年九月来中国的。
Wǒ shì qùnián jiǔyuè lái Zhōngguó de.
I came to China last September.

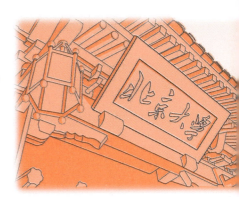

男1： 你在中国学习汉语吗?
Nǐ zài Zhōngguó xuéxí Hànyǔ ma?
Are you studying Chinese in China?

男2： 我在北京大学学习汉语。
Wǒ zài Běijīng Dàxué xuéxí Hànyǔ.
I am studying Chinese at Peking University.

男1： 你为什么要学习汉语?
Nǐ wèi shénme yào xuéxí Hànyǔ?
Why do you want to learn Chinese?

男2： 因为我喜欢中国历史,我希望看懂中文书。
Yīnwèi wǒ xǐhuan Zhōngguó lìshǐ, wǒ xīwàng kàndǒng Zhōngwén shū.
Because I like Chinese history and I wish to be able to read Chinese books.

男1： 现在你的汉语水平怎么样？
Xiànzài nǐ de Hànyǔ shuǐpíng zěnmeyàng?
How is your Chinese at present?

男2： 还不太好，还看不懂中文报纸。
Hái bú tài hǎo, hái kàn bu dǒng Zhōngwén bàozhǐ.
Not so good. I cannot read Chinese newspaper yet.

男1： 读报是学习汉语的好办法，你应该开始看报纸。
Dú bào shì xuéxí Hànyǔ de hǎo bànfǎ, nǐ yīnggāi kāishǐ kàn bàozhǐ.
Reading newspaper is a good way to learn Chinese. You should start reading newspapers.

男2： 我打算上读报课，我们学校有这门课。
Wǒ dǎsuan shàng dú bào kè, wǒmen xuéxiào yǒu zhè mén kè.
I plan to attend the course of newspaper reading. Our school offers this course.

男1： 那好极了！
Nà hǎo jí le!
That is great!

男2： 我一定读得很慢。
Wǒ yídìng dú de hěn màn.
I must be very slow in reading.

男1： 不要紧，每个人开始的时候都很慢。
Bú yàojǐn, měi gè rén kāishǐ de shíhou dōu hěn màn.
It does not matter. Everybody starts slowly.

15 我的中文进步很快
My Chinese Standard Improves Rapidly

(二)

女： 你在干什么？
Nǐ zài gàn shénme?
What are you doing?

男： 我正在看报纸呢！
Wǒ zhèngzài kàn bàozhǐ ne!
I am reading newspaper!

女： 中文报还是英文报？
Zhōngwén bào háishì Yīngwén bào?
Is it Chinese newspaper or English newspaper?

男： 中文报，是《人民日报》。
Zhōngwén bào, shì 《Rénmín Rìbào》.
Chinese newspaper. It is the *People's Daily*.

女： 你能看懂《人民日报》了，太好了！
Nǐ néng kàndǒng 《Rénmín Rìbào》 le, tài hǎo le!
It is great you can understand the *People's Daily*!

男： 我一边查字典，一边看报纸，很慢。
Wǒ yìbiān chá zìdiǎn, yìbiān kàn bàozhǐ, hěn màn.
I refer to the dictionary while reading, so it goes on very slowly.

女： 你是什么时候开始看中文报纸的？
Nǐ shì shénme shíhou kāishǐ kàn Zhōngwén bàozhǐ de?
When did you begin to read Chinese newspaper?

男： 是昨天开始的。
Shì zuótiān kāishǐ de.
I began yesterday.

女：你学习真努力！
Nǐ xuéxí zhēn nǔlì!
How hard you work!

（三）读报的好处
The advantages of reading newspapers

看报纸有很多好处。看了报纸，你可以了解国际新闻，你可以知道中国国内大事；你能看到旅游介绍，你会知道商品的信息；你还可以了解哪儿有音乐会，哪个饭店的饭菜味道最好，怎样保持身体健康，怎样减肥，明天会不会下雨……什么信息都有。

除了这些好处，读报还有一个最大的好处——帮助我学习中文。因为我天天看报纸，所以我的中文水平进步很快。现在我已经可以看懂中文历史书了，我还能看中文电视呢！

There are a lot of advantages of newspaper reading. You can learn about both international news and domestic affairs. You can read about tourism services and commodity news. You can also get the information about where to go for concerts and which restaurant provides delicious dish; how to keep healthy, how to go on a diet, or if it is going to rain tomorrow, etc.

Besides all these, reading newspaper has the biggest advantage—it helps me with my Chinese study. Thanks to my daily

15 我的中文进步很快
My Chinese Standard Improves Rapidly

newspaper reading, my Chinese standard improves rapidly. I am able to read books on Chinese history now. I can also understand some Chinese TV programs.

注释 | Annotation

1. 我希望看懂中文书。I hope I can read Chinese books.
   你能看到旅游介绍。You can see the introduction of tourist.

   "看懂、看到"是两个结果补语式，动词"懂"和"到"分别出现在"看"后，补充说明看的结果。

   "看懂" and "看到", are two forms of verbs followed by a complement indicating the result of the action.

2. 还看不懂中文报纸。I can not read Chinese newspaper yet.

   表示"还不能看中文报纸"。在结果补语式的动词和补语之间加上"得"和"不"就构成可能补语式，表示可能性。如：看得懂/看不懂。如：

   This sentence means "can not read Chinese newspaper yet". The insertion of "得" or "不" between the verb and the complement indicates possibility. Such as "看得懂"/"看不懂". For example:

   （1）听得懂／听不懂

   　　　to be able to comprehend/not to be able to comprehend

(2) 学得会 / 学不会

to be able to learn/ not be able to learn

语法 | Grammar

1. 呢

"呢"有三个作用：（1）表示疑问："我喜欢吃辣的，你呢？"（2）表示动作正在进行："我正在看报呢！"（3）表示确定的语气："我还能看电视呢！"

There are three functions of "呢"：（1）to indicate an interrogative tone："我喜欢吃辣的，你呢？"（I like spicy food, how about you?）（2）to indicate an action is in process："我正在看报呢！"（I am reading newspaper.）(3)to indicate an affirmative tone："我还能看电视呢！"（I can even watch and understand the TV program.）

2. 因为……所以……

表示原因和结果。如：

This is a structure of expressing cause and result. For example:

(1) 我因为病了，所以没去上课。

I do not go to school because I am ill.

(2) 因为天气不好，所以我没去锻炼。

I stop the physical exercise because of the bad weather.

15 我的中文进步很快
My Chinese Standard Improves Rapidly

练习 | Exercises

1. 听录音，选择合适的回答：

Listen to the record and choose a proper answer:

(1) A. 我是去年来的。
　　B. 我是一个人来的。
　　C. 我是坐飞机来的。

(2) A. 我喜欢中国历史。
　　B. 我打算上读报课。
　　C. 还不太好，还不能看中文报纸。

(3) A. 可以了解国际新闻。
　　B. 一边查字典，一边看报纸。
　　C. 一定读得很慢。

(4) A. 不，我看得懂。
　　B. 我还看不懂。
　　C. 看中文报纸有很多好处。

2. 选词填空：

Choose the right words to fill in the following blanks:

　　看懂　　听懂　　看到　　住满　　卖完　　打开

(1) 对不起，双人房间都（　　）了。
(2) 请（　　）书。
(3) 我说中文，你能（　　）吗？

（4）你（　　）那个消息了吗？

（5）我已经能（　　）中文书了！

（6）对不起，那本书（　　）了。

3. 替换练习：

Substitution exercises:

（1）你买得到 火车票吗？

　　　学得好　中文

　　　打得好　网球

　　　看得到　外边的风景

（2）我看不懂《人民日报》。

　　　弹不好　钢琴

　　　买不到　那本字典

　　　学不会　游泳

4. 回答问题：

Answer the following questions:

（1）你是什么时候出生的？

（2）音乐会是几点的？

（3）你是什么时候开始读《人民日报》的？

（4）他是什么时候去商店的？

15 我的中文进步很快
My Chinese Standard Improves Rapidly

5. 连词成句：

Make sentences:

（1）是　好办法　读报　汉语　学习　的

_____

（2）天天　因为　报纸　所以　看　进步　中文　很快

_____

（3）希望　我　经常　国际　了解　大事　国内　和

_____

（4）常常　一边　看　查　报纸　字典　我　一边

_____

（5）我　看懂　现在　已经　了　历史　中文　书　可以

_____

6. 用下列词语续写：

Complete this passage with the following words:

　　学习汉语有很多好处。……　除了这些好处，学习汉语还有一个最大的好处……

　　参考词语：了解　知道　中国　历史　旅游　信息
　　　　　　　报纸　电视　新闻

生词 | New Words

| 1 | 时候 | shíhou | （名） | time | 小时候 / childhood time
春天的时候 / spring time
你什么时候来中国的？
What time did you come to China? |

2	大学	dàxué	(名)	university	一所(suǒ, measure word)大学 a university 上大学 / study at a university 我在北京大学学习。 I'm studying at Peking University.
3	报纸	bàozhǐ	(名)	newspaper	看报纸 / read newspaper 中文报纸 / Chinese newspaper 我看不懂中文报纸。 I can not understand Chinese newspaper.
4	新闻	xīnwén	(名)	news	看新闻 / watch news 了解新闻 / understand news 每天晚上我们都看国际新闻。 Every night we watch international news.
5	国内	guónèi	(名)	domestic	国内新闻 / domestic news 国内大事 / domestic big events 他在国内学习。 He is studying in the domestic country.
6	商品	shāngpǐn	(名)	commodity	一件(jiàn, measure word)商品 a piece of commodity 商品价格 the price of the commodity 商店里有各种各样的商品。 There are different kinds of commodities in the store.
7	信息	xìnxī	(名)	information	商品信息 / commodity information 我告诉了他一个信息。 I told him a piece of information.
8	进步	jìnbù	(动)	to improve	很大的进步 great improvement 进步很快 / fast improvement 我的汉语进步了。 I have got improvement on the Chinese.

15 我的中文进步很快
My Chinese Standard Improves Rapidly

9	去年	qùnián	（名）	last year	去年七月 / July of last year 我是去年上大学的。 I went to college last year. 去年秋天我去了上海。 I went to Shanghai last autumn.
10	查	chá	（动）	to check; to look up (dictionary)	查字典 / look up dictionary 查资料(zīliào, material) check materials 不懂就应该去查字典。 Look up dictionary if you do not understand.
11	字典	zìdiǎn	（名）	dictionary	一本字典 / a dictionary 汉语字典 / Chinese dictionary 这个字我也不认识，你查查字典吧。 I do not know this word. Please look up dictionary.

听力录音文本及参考答案

1. （1）你是什么时候来中国的？
   （2）现在你的汉语水平怎么样？
   （3）看报纸有什么好处？
   （4）你能看懂中文报纸吗？
   （1）A　（2）C　（3）A　（4）B

2. （1）住满　（2）打开　（3）听懂　（4）看到　（5）看懂　（6）卖完

3. 略。

4. 略。

5. （1）读报是学习汉语的好办法。
   （2）因为天天看中文报纸，所以进步很快。
   （3）我希望经常了解国际和国内大事。
   （4）我常常一边看报纸一边查字典。
   （5）现在我已经可以看懂中文历史书了。

6. 略。

生词总表
Vocabulary

	A	
爱好者	àihàozhě	13

	B	
百	bǎi	5
办法	bànfǎ	10
棒球	bàngqiú	13
饱	bǎo	7
保持	bǎochí	10
报纸	bàozhǐ	15
北	běi	4
北边	běibian	4
比	bǐ	8
比较	bǐjiào	9
变成	biànchéng	9
冰箱	bīngxiāng	6
不过	búguò	2

	C	
才	cái	2
菜	cài	11
菜单	càidān	11
餐厅	cāntīng	3
操场	cāochǎng	13
查	chá	15
产品	chǎnpǐn	14
长	cháng	2
橙汁	chéngzhī	11
吃	chī	3
出口	chūkǒu	14
出生	chūshēng	2
除了	chúle	1
穿	chuān	8
春天	chūntiān	9
次	cì	5
从来	cónglái	13

	D	
达到	dádào	14
打$_1$	dǎ	6
打$_2$	dǎ	13
大学	dàxué	15
大约	dàyuē	2
得	dé	13
低	dī	9
第一	dìyī	10
电话	diànhuà	6

生词总表 Vocabulary

电脑	diànnǎo	3
电视	diànshì	6
东	dōng	4
东西	dōngxi	4
动物	dòngwù	4
动物园	dòngwùyuán	4
豆腐	dòufu	11
度	dù	9
短	duǎn	8
锻炼	duànliàn	10
对面	duìmiàn	4
顿	dùn	12
多$_1$	duō	1
多$_2$	duō	13

F

发烧	fā shāo	10
饭	fàn	3
放假	fàng jià	3
分钟	fēnzhōng	4
风景	fēngjǐng	5
附近	fùjìn	4

G

高	gāo	9
告诉	gàosu	4
各	gè	4
给	gěi	7
工作	gōngzuò	2
公园	gōngyuán	4
够	gòu	5
够	gòu	9
贵姓	guìxìng	1
国	guó	1
国际	guójì	6
国内	guónèi	15

H

孩子	háizi	9
好处	hǎochù	1
好看	hǎokàn	8
好玩儿	hǎowánr	4
合作	hézuò	14
后天	hòutiān	5
滑冰	huá bīng	13
黄	huáng	8
活动	huódòng	13
火车	huǒchē	5
或者	huòzhě	10

J

鸡蛋	jīdàn	11
季节	jìjié	9
继续	jìxù	3
价格	jiàgé	14
减肥	jiǎn féi	12
件	jiàn	8
渐渐	jiànjiàn	9
饺子	jiǎozi	7
介绍	jièshào	14

223

今年	jīnnián	2
进步	jìnbù	15
进口	jìnkǒu	14
精神	jīngshén	10
酒	jiǔ	7
旧	jiù	8
决定	juédìng	12

K		
开	kāi	9
开始	kāishǐ	2
咳嗽	késou	10
可是	kěshì	12
客人	kèrén	1
课	kè	3
空调	kōngtiáo	6
口袋	kǒudai	6
快	kuài	3

L		
辣	là	11
辣子鸡丁	làzi jīdīng	11
劳驾	láojià	5
老板	lǎobǎn	1
累	lèi	10
里	lǐ	6
量	liáng	10
楼	lóu	6
旅行	lǚxíng	5
旅游	lǚyóu	9

M		
麻辣豆腐	málà dòufu	11
马上	mǎshàng	11
卖	mài	5
卖掉	màidiào	8
忙	máng	10
没有	méiyǒu	12
门	mén	3
米饭	mǐfàn	11
面	miàn	6
明天	míngtiān	5

N		
南	nán	4
南边	nánbian	4
年轻	niánqīng	13
牛排	niúpái	6
暖和	nuǎnhuo	9

P		
胖	pàng	12
跑步	pǎo bù	12
便宜	piányi	3
票	piào	5
漂亮	piàoliang	7
瓶	píng	7

Q		
起床	qǐ chuáng	2

生词总表 Vocabulary

气温	qìwēn	9
请	qǐng	2
秋天	qiūtiān	9
去年	qùnián	15
裙子	qúnzi	8

R

日	rì	2

S

商品	shāngpǐn	15
上	shàng	5
上午	shàngwǔ	3
少	shǎo	12
生产	shēngchǎn	14
生气	shēng qì	10
生日	shēngrì	2
时候	shíhou	15
瘦	shòu	12
书店	shūdiàn	9
树	shù	9
谁	shuí	1
水	shuǐ	10
水果	shuǐguǒ	7
水平	shuǐpíng	14
睡觉	shuì jiào	2
顺着	shùnzhe	4
说明书	shuōmíng	14
送	sòng	7
素菜	sùcài	11
酸	suān	11
随便	suíbiàn	7
岁	suì	2

T

她	tā	1
太极拳	tàijíquán	13
太阳	tàiyáng	9
汤	tāng	11
糖醋鱼	tángcùyú	11
讨论	tǎolùn	14
体操	tǐcāo	12
体温	tǐwēn	10
体育	tǐyù	13
天	tiān	1
条	tiáo	4
停止	tíngzhǐ	13
图书馆	túshūguǎn	3

W

外边	wàibian	9
完	wán	2
玩	wán	7
碗	wǎn	11
网球	wǎngqiú	13
味道	wèidào	11
温和	wēnhé	9
问题	wèntí	14

无论	wúlùn	13

X		
西	xī	4
西边	xībian	4
西餐厅	xīcāntīng	6
西药	xīyào	10
希望	xīwàng	14
洗	xǐ	6
先进	xiānjìn	14
咸	xián	11
小	xiǎo	8
小时	xiǎoshí	3
些	xiē	7
新	xīn	8
新闻	xīnwén	15
信息	xìnxī	15
姓	xìng	1
熊猫	xióngmāo	4
学期	xuéqī	3
学校	xuéxiào	3

Y		
颜色	yánsè	8
阳光	yángguāng	9
样	yàng	13
样品	yàngpǐn	14
样子	yàngzi	8
药	yào	10

要紧	yàojǐn	10
一般	yìbān	2
一边	yìbiān	6
一定	yídìng	7
一下	yíxià	14
衣服	yīfu	6
已经	yǐjīng	7
以前	yǐqián	14
游泳	yóuyǒng	13
有的	yǒude	8
有名	yǒumíng	11
又	yòu	7
鱼	yú	11
愉快	yúkuài	10
雨水	yǔshuǐ	9
语言	yǔyán	1
原谅	yuánliàng	1
月	yuè	2
越来越	yuèláiyuè	12

Z		
早	zǎo	1
早上	zǎoshang	1
张	zhāng	5
着	zhe	6
这儿	zhèr	6
这里	zhèlǐ	11
这么	zhème	12
真	zhēn	4

只	zhǐ	4
质量	zhìliàng	14
中(号)	zhōng(hào)	8
中餐厅	zhōngcāntīng	6
中午	zhōngwǔ	3
中药	zhōngyào	10
注意	zhùyì	10

字典	zìdiǎn	15
最近	zuìjìn	10
昨天	zuótiān	9
作用	zuòyòng	12
坐	zuò	5
座位	zuòwèi	11

专有名词
Proper Nouns

	D	
德语	Déyǔ	1

	F	
法国	Fǎguó	1
法国人	Fǎguórén	6
法语	Fǎyǔ	1

	L	
李英	Lǐ Yīng	1

	M	
马学文	Mǎ Xuéwén	2
美国人	Měiguórén	1

	P	
平田	Píngtián	14

	R	
日本	Rìběn	1
日本人	Rìběnrén	6
日语	Rìyǔ	1

	S	
上海	Shànghǎi	5
四川	Sìchuān	11

	Y	
意大利	Yìdàlì	6
意大利人	Yìdàlìrén	6
英国	Yīngguó	1
英国人	Yīngguórén	1
英语	Yīngyǔ	1

附录
Appendix

Gǔ Shī Sān Shǒu
古诗三首
Three Ancient Poems

唐 代（Tang Dynasty）
Táng Dài

李 白（701—762）
Lǐ Bái

SEEING MENG HAORAN OFF AT YELLOW CRANE TOWER

My friend has left the west where the Yellow Crane towers

For River Town green with willows and red with flowers.

His lessening sail is lost in the boundless blue sky,

Where I see but the endless River rolling by.

唐　代（Tang Dynasty）
Táng Dài

孟　郊（751—814）
Mèng Jiāo

游子吟
yóu zǐ yín

慈母手中线，
cí mǔ shǒu zhōng xiàn,

游子身上衣。
yóu zǐ shēn shàng yī.

临行密密缝，
lín xíng mì mi féng,

意恐迟迟归。
yì kǒng chí chí guī.

谁言寸草心，
shuí yán cùn cǎo xīn,

报得三春晖。
bào dé sān chūn huī.

SONG OF THE PARTING SON

The thread in mother's hand-
A grown for parting son,
Sewn stitch by stitch, alas!
For fear of cold he'll stand.
Such kindness of warm sun
Can't be repaid by grass.

宋　代（Song Dynasty）
Sòng Dài

欧阳　修（1007—1072）
Ōuyáng Xiū

丰　乐　亭　游　春
fēng　lè　tíng　yóu　chūn

红　树　青　山　日　欲　斜，
hóng　shù　qīng　shān　rì　yù　xié
长　郊　草　色　绿　无　涯。
cháng　jiāo　cǎo　sè　lǜ　wú　yá
游　人　不　管　春　将　老，
yóu　rén　bù　guǎn　chūn　jiāng　lǎo
来　往　亭　前　踏　落　花。
lái　wǎng　tíng　qián　tà　luò　huā

BEFORE THE PAVILION

The mountains green are dappled with red leaves, behold!
At sunset out of sight the verdant meadows spread.
Visitors do not care that spring will soon grow old;
On fallen blooms before the pavilion they tread.